Eating for Beginners

Books by Melanie Rehak

Girl Sleuth:
Nancy Drew and the Women Who Created Her

Eating for Beginners:
An Education in the Pleasures of Food from
Chefs, Farmers, and One Picky Kid

Eating for Beginners

An Education in
the Pleasures of Food
from Chefs, Farmers,
and One Picky Kid

MELANIE REHAK

HOUGHTON MIFFLIN HARCOURT

BOSTON · NEW YORK

2010

www.hmhbooks.com

Library of Congress Cataloging-in-Publication Data
Rehak, Melanie.
Eating for beginners : an education in the pleasures of food
from chefs, farmers, and one picky kid / Melanie Rehak.
p. cm.
ISBN 978-0-15-101437-8
1. Gastronomy. 2. Cookery. 3. Applewood Restaurant
(Brooklyn, New York, N.Y.) 4. Rehak, Melanie. I. Title.
TX633.R45 2010
641'.013—dc22   2009047467

Book design by Victoria Hartman

Printed in the United States of America

DOC 10 9 8 7 6 5 4 3 2 1

Lines from "A Winter's Tale" by Wyatt Prunty appear courtesy of the author. "A Little
Madness in the Spring" is reprinted by permission of the publishers and the Trustees of
Amherst College from *The Poems of Emily Dickinson*, Thomas H. Johnson, editor, Cam-
bridge, Mass.: The Belknap Press of Harvard University Press, copyright © 1951, 1955,
1979, 1983 by the President and Fellows of Harvard College. Lines from "Variations: The
Air Is Sweetest That a Thistle Guards," edited by J. D. McClatchy and Stephen Yenser,
copyright © 2001 by the Literary Estate of James Merrill at Washington University, from
Collected Poems by James Merrill, edited by J. D. McClatchy and Stephen Yenser. Used
by permission of Alfred A. Knopf, a division of Random House, Inc. Lines from "Reluc-
tance" from *The Poetry of Robert Frost*, edited by Edward Connery Lathem. Copyright
© 1934, 1969 by Henry Holt and Company. Copyright 1962 by Robert Frost. Reprinted
by arrangement with Henry Holt and Company, LLC.

To protect the privacy of individuals, pseudonyms are used
for the kitchen staff at applewood restaurant.

for Noah

My subject is my place in the world.

— WENDELL BERRY

Contents

Eating for Beginners

Introduction

A few months after my son Jules turned one, I started working in the kitchen of a small restaurant down the street from
my apartment in Brooklyn, New York, called applewood
(the lowercase *a* being a choice the owners hoped would
convey plenty in contrast to the sharp, aggressive point
of the capital *A* they had forgone). This unexpected move
prompted various raised eyebrows and one miscommunica-
tion that resulted in several of my husband Noah's friends
thinking I had gone belly up as a writer and needed alternate
employment to help keep the family afloat. At a moment
when many new mothers marvel at how quickly time passes
or weep over outgrown onesies and booties, I instead en-
deavored to become, as the great food writer M. F. K. Fisher
referred to herself in 1943, "the gastronomical me."

It was not, however, because I felt pangs of longing for
the tiny (screaming, incomprehensible) baby who was gone

forever. Nor did I do it because I had long harbored a secret desire to be on *Top Chef*, win thanks to my brilliant use of okra in all five courses of a meal including dessert, and open my own restaurant in a blaze of media glory.

I did it because I needed an education. The one I already had, which had served me quite well for some decades both professionally and personally, had lately begun to seem outdated. This was partly because of Jules. Though no one tells you until after the fact, every new parent experiences some variation of this feeling: one day you're a responsible adult with a clear grip on the details of your life and how they function; the next, you wake up to whole constellations of problems that you've not only never dealt with before, but had no idea even existed—exploding diapers, sleep schedules, an ever-present epaulet of spit-up on all your shirts that you don't notice until you've already left the house, and so on. And in spite of the host of experts (and their books and magazine articles and web sites) who seem to arrive with every new baby in the twenty-first century, there is always a question hovering in the air: Which of these things—you and the baby sleeping, you and the baby wearing clean clothes, you and the baby doing or not doing something you don't even know about yet—actually matter?

And then Jules grew old enough to eat solid food. Just as I was moving out of the confusion about layering his clothing and teething signs and why he crawled backwards first, I encountered a whole new set of choices I was unequipped to make. In short: What was he supposed to eat?

This was a question I had already been asking myself for

some time, and it represented the other area in which my education seemed to be failing me. Eating, as it happened, was a subject in which I had been interested long before having a baby. Before I ever cracked any books with titles like *The Seven Sleep Habits of Highly Effective Infants,* I was cuddling up at night with Julia Child and James Beard and Mark Bittman and falling asleep with visions of roasts and sautés dancing in my head. None of which is to say that I was a genius in the kitchen. I was a pretty good cook if not necessarily an inspired one. I was game for almost anything and I liked to throw dinner parties, but I was also happy eating an egg-and-cheese sandwich from a cart on the street. I patronized greenmarkets and was (and am) a long-time fan of numerous unpopular vegetables, like Brussels sprouts, though I didn't (and don't) expect others to be since I personally can't stand melon of any kind.

But then, somewhere in the few years before Jules was born, my feelings about food started to change. Along with Child and Beard and Bittman, I had begun reading Michael Pollan and Eric Schlosser and Wendell Berry. Initially, I wasn't sure I wanted to—I feared being lectured about what I was eating and then feeling even more guiltily ignorant than before. I resisted buying *Fast Food Nation* for several years, but when I finally did start it, the book quickly won me over. Not only were my concerns about its tone unfounded, but it was a pleasure to read. I was actually relieved that the train I was on when I first opened it stalled for three hours, allowing me a chunk of uninterrupted reading time. There were no lectures, only useful information and engaging narratives.

Next came Pollan's *The Omnivore's Dilemma* and *In Defense of Food*, and after that Berry's *What Are People For?* Together, these books presented, much as my child did, a host of issues that I was first unaware of and then unsure how to prioritize—issues that often left me paralyzed in front of a produce or dairy or meat display at a supermarket or greenmarket. What, exactly, was I supposed to be buying?

I knew that I should be eating less meat. Pollan's intentionally simple motto had stuck with me as it had with so many other people: "Eat food. Not too much. Mostly plants." But when I *did* eat meat, I still didn't know what kind it should be. Was grass-fed more important than organic or vice versa? And what if I didn't have access to either? What about food miles and growth hormones and climate change and land preservation? Maybe it would be easier to give up meat altogether.

I also knew I should avoid processed food. (*Fast Food Nation* permanently destroyed my love of McDonald's French fries, and for about a week after I finished it I couldn't even walk by a food store without feeling both slightly nauseated and suspicious about the origins and production of every item on display.) But there were moments when doing so seemed impossible or just hugely inconvenient, and other moments when, to be honest, I just didn't want to. I wanted to think a little more about what I ate and why, but I couldn't keep up with all the information coming my way, important and well intended as it was, and as a result I simply blocked a good deal of it out.

Which, I should say, was no easy feat. Every newspaper

or magazine I picked up seemed to have a story about people who ate only certain foods or cut out certain other foods for health reasons, political reasons, or environmental reasons. One study I came across claimed that sixty-one percent of Americans were confused about what to feed their families. I found that depressing but was also relieved to know I wasn't alone. Clearly the old methods of learning about food have been made obsolete by everything from enormous changes in agricultural practices to modern technology and the work schedules it has brought with it. As children, many people I know, myself included, rode in the seats of grocery carts on weekends, watching their mothers and fathers buy food at the nearest market (and pestering them for candy). Now, even if you do still engage in the receding practice of shopping for groceries in person instead of online, the odds that you'll be able to teach your child anything during those visits are pretty slim; you'll be too busy debating whether or not paying the extra two dollars per half gallon for hormone-free milk is worth giving up something else on your grocery list. (For the record, I happen to think it is.)

Since I was now in charge of steering the cart (and saying no to the candy), I thought I'd better sort out a few matters to pass on to my son. If the lettuce I bought was organic but came from California, was I saying I cared more about what I put into my body than I did about fuel consumption and global warming? If I chose chicken that was hormone-free but not free-range, was there any point? Was it really so bad to eat a hot dog once in a while? One thing I knew for certain: I was not about to give up my favorite Austrian cookies. I felt vaguely distressed that I refused to allow my panic about the world's dependence on oil stand in the way of re-visiting many happy childhood afternoons by eating hazel-nut wafers, but there it was.

What really happened when Jules got old enough to eat, in other words, was the unavoidable collision of two worlds of information—parenting and eating. To begin with, there, in the form of my baby son, was an actual person for whom I wanted to leave the planet in decent condition. That goal was no longer just a noble abstraction. Then there was the amaz-ing fact that I had before me in a highchair someone who had literally never tasted anything, whose body had yet to be tainted by MSG in bad Chinese take-out, or clogged by palm oil "butter" on movie theater popcorn, or compromised by pesticide residue. I was unprepared for both the sheer weird-ness of this—was it possible that I actually knew a person who had never eaten chocolate?—and the huge responsibility I felt to get it right. Yet I couldn't imagine not feeding Jules the things—okay, the hazelnut wafers—that had brought me joy as a child, even though many of them were imported over long distances and very sugary. Some part of me resented the fact that something that should have been a pure pleasure, teaching a person to eat, was now so complicated.

One moment stands out. It was around five in the morning on a raw midwinter day when Jules was about eight months old. He was an extremely early riser, clearly a genetic anom-aly (I myself am famous for having slept through the night on my second day home from the hospital). True to form that morning, I was lying just this side of comatose on the kitchen floor in my bathrobe, watching him crawl around happily after the Cheerios I had scattered all over the room. This setup was one of my main parenting accomplishments to date. I had discovered that if I set him free on this mission, he would be both fed and occupied without my having to move much at all. Occasionally he would crawl over to me, offer me a Cheerio, and then stuff it gleefully into his own mouth before scrambling off to find the next one. (When I described this scenario to an acquaintance whose son was a bit older than Jules, instead of the sympathetic smile I expected she gave me an odd sideways look and then, obviously choosing her words with the utmost care, said slowly, "That's a funny story," in a tone that made it clear she didn't think it was funny at all and was considering calling Child Protective Services.)

So there I was, contemplating mustering up the effort to press the "brew" button on the coffeemaker as Jules scuttled around, when the knowing recent words of a friend popped, unbidden, into my mind. "The organic Cheerios are best."

All of a sudden my morning routine, so elegant in its energy-saving simplicity, was blown to bits. My Cheerios, naturally, were not organic. Rather than life-saving little circles, they now appeared quite suspect. The General Mills logo on the screaming yellow box looked like nothing so much as a sinister black sneer. I was totally sleep-deprived, but still able, somehow, to feel bad about what I was feeding my child. (As for the issue of whether or not my floor was clean enough to lie on, much less eat off of, well, let's just say that this is a book about food, not hygiene. And also that I was more than willing to trade a certain amount of risk in one area for a certain amount of rest in another.)

But there was a light in the foodie darkness, and unexpectedly it emanated from a restaurant devoted to local farmers and sustainable agriculture: this was applewood. David and Laura Shea, who own the restaurant where I eventually landed in the kitchen, believe fiercely in these principles and yet are all about the joy of both cooking and food. They don't fetishize food or lecture their patrons about it; they do what they need to in order to feel good about their business and their own lives, but if you just want to eat dinner, it's okay by them. Humanity, in the deepest sense of the word, matters to them as much as ideology. As David explained to me, when you run a restaurant you're in the business of catering to people's desires. You can give them access to their fondest memories simply by serving them a meal. What that means is that at certain moments you give in and order a flat of strawberries from California because the weather has turned warm and it's strawberry season in the heart and mind even if it isn't on the East Coast of the United States.

In addition to having made sense of all of this for themselves, the Sheas were also somehow managing to stick to their principles and run the restaurant while raising two daughters: Tatum, born just a few weeks after applewood opened in 2004, and Sophie, who had been three at the time.

So it was Laura's voice that interrupted my guilty musings that cold morning as I pondered the box of Cheerios—the voice of a parent who knew all about what food could and should be but also knew that, as I was fast learning, being a parent, just like being committed to sustainable agriculture or eating locally, sometimes means figuring out what you think is right and then facing reality.

"The first time I saw Sophie eating Cheetos, a part of me died a little inside," Laura once confessed to me. "But I didn't say anything and I was very proud of myself. You can't always be championing a cause. Don't you sometimes just want to have a Snickers bar and call it a day?" She had paused for a moment and then said thoughtfully, "I'm realizing it's evolutionary. Where I am now is different from where I was a year ago or a year before that."

Yes, I thought on that cold winter morning, lolling on the floor amid the Cheerios as the sun finally came up. I will evolve.

Which was how I found myself, a few months later, in the kitchen at applewood, wearing a chef's jacket, with many long days and nights of cooking ahead of me. After that came some very early mornings (my favorite) and long days working on some of the local farms that supplied the kitchen. If I was really going to learn about food, if I was going to understand the choices and the compromises for myself and be able to make them with confidence, I wanted to learn about it from, quite literally, the ground up. I wanted to understand, finally, who (besides Joel Salatin, the farmer featured in *The Omnivore's Dilemma* and later in the documentary

Food, Inc.) was behind the phrase "local farmer" and who, exactly, got the food these farmers grew to those of us who were supposedly so concerned about it. I wanted, I confess, to butcher a pig. So I went to the barns and the fields and the restaurant kitchen, and I started over.

Then, just as I was embarking on my new food life at applewood, Jules became a child who, despite being born of a mother who once ate goat brains in Marrakech and a father who would happily live on kimchee and innards of innumerable varieties, wouldn't eat anything. He wouldn't eat eggs, meat of any kind, or cheese. Or pasta. Or toast. Yes, I said toast. In light of this (I know: toast), I suddenly felt that—all politics aside—it would be pure heaven to prepare food that would actually be appreciated by people who would actually eat it when it was served. People who would not throw it to the ground shouting "Da! Da! Da!" and demand yogurt for supper. And so, in addition to being the place where I learned about the pleasures and aesthetics and complications of cooking with local food and changing the menu daily, the place where I may have worked harder than ever before in my life, applewood became for me something all parents of small children secretly long for on occasion, even though we're never supposed to admit it: an escape.

I began this project with a lot of other people's ideas about food in my head—including what I've proved beyond a doubt to be the entirely false one that if you just offer children a variety of food, they'll eat it (some children will, of course, but definitely not mine). By the end, I had my own ideas. I let the food itself and the people who produce and cook it, rather than the hype surrounding it, teach me. No one I met told me what to eat. They told me what *they* eat—both bad and good—and they told me why they think about food the way they do. Knowing that each of them, from the chefs to the farmers to the distributors, had committed his or her life to food in a way I have not, I weighed their experiences and then I made sure I understood the other side of their arguments, too. Among other things, I learned how much work it takes from numerous people to make it possible to eat something as simple as a salad of local lettuce with beets and goat cheese, and that new knowledge permanently changed the way I see that salad. I also learned that even the most devoted among us still buy food that isn't local or organic because to be human means to be an eater and to seek solace or delectation in food from time to time, regardless of its origins or composition.

I picked produce at a farm upstate, I made cheese, I worked many ten-hour shifts in the applewood kitchen (and watched David do the same after being up all night with one or both of his daughters). I rode through the night in a delivery truck after packing produce for hours in a frigid cooler room. I milked goats and went fifty miles out to sea on a fishing boat. These experiences taught me repeatedly that knowing something is true—we should eat as locally as possible, we should support small farms—and understanding *why* it's true are two very different things. They also taught me about the pleasure, as opposed to the duty, in making these choices.

Meanwhile my son, inveterate tosser of plates and refuser of cheeses, taught me that knowing what your child should eat—variety, organic—is useless in a face-off with a willful toddler, and that accepting that truth, just like eating the occasional strawberry in winter, has its place.

Like parenting, eating in twenty-first-century America is riddled with choices, challenges, great joy, and utter confusion. There's no single right way to do either one, but if you're lucky, you can learn to accept both on their own terms and live with the surprising results. On my first day in the kitchen at applewood, awed and daunted by all the French terminology (*chinois*, anyone?) and the gigantic utensils being thrown around, I was asked to pick herb leaves from their stems for garnishes. I sorted tarragon and chervil into white plastic containers that would be part of the *mise en place*—the ingredients prepared in advance for the chef's use—near the grill. With the seriousness I thought befitted the moments just before dinner service began, I handed the fresh green leaves to David and watched him line them up with the rest of the evening's necessities, which were in cylindrical plastic quarts on a bed of ice.

Then I noticed, next to the herbs I'd just sorted and the finely minced chives and flaky sea salt, a glistening pile of orange, red, yellow, and green Sour Patch Kids in an identical container. "Dig in!" David said to me, throwing a few into his mouth and turning back to the stove. And so I did.

1

❖

In the Beginning

THIS IS HOW you butcher a duck. Make a slit down one side of its backbone, then insert your knife and scrape down carefully along the breastbone, swinging the tip of the knife in smooth arcs while pulling the breast meat away with your other hand as it comes loose. When it's free, slice it off. Repeat on the other side. Trim off fat, sinew and vein. These will be everywhere. Things will be slippery. You could make the wrong cut. When the breasts are trimmed and set aside, remove each leg from the body by bending it back and cutting through the joint. You will feel as if you're wrestling with someone covered in oil. Put the legs aside for confit. Then stand up the carcass and, with a big cleaver, chop it down the center so it falls into two pieces. Cut each piece crosswise. Put the four pieces in a pan and into the oven to roast for stock. Repeat with nine more ducks until the breasts are coming off a little less raggedly and you think you may be getting the hang of it.

The next day, try to trim your one-year-old's fingernails. Things will be slippery. You could make the wrong cut. You will feel as if you're wrestling with someone—a small someone—covered in oil. As you try to hold him still, reflect that it was much easier to cut his nails when he was a newborn and couldn't move, then on the startling fact that a duck is about the same size as a newborn. Realize with surprise that you genuinely feel it's easier to butcher a duck, something you had never done before yesterday, than to give a one-year-old a nail trim. Realize, too, that your life since you became a parent has been one long learning curve with no end in sight. That you long for a sense of accomplishment and that maybe butchering ducks is a way to get it. Scrape, slice, trim, cut, chop, and you're done. When a duck is butchered, it's butchered.

In the applewood kitchen there is no busywork. Just as there is no unusable part of a bird or other animal, no fruit or vegetable too unfamiliar to cook with, so there is no time wasted, no resource untapped—not even the amateur on her first day. I was there to serve my own purposes—I had suggested the arrangement, which involved a few days a week at the start but grew to include more later on, and was still somewhat amazed at the ease with which David had agreed—and I was not being paid because I was, after all, researching a book for which I *had* been paid. But from the moment I arrived at one o'clock for my first dinner shift and was told to go downstairs to the lockers and change into a chef's jacket and pants (which in my mind was tantamount to impersonation and thus probably a crime in at least a few states), it was terrifyingly clear to me that I was going to serve David's purposes as well. That is, I was going to cook, which seemed reasonable except that it meant the food I prepared would be served in the dining room that very evening. In a matter of hours, I would be transformed from a person accustomed to watching the food she offered either go untouched or get thrown on the floor to one making food for paying customers—people who sat on the other side of the swinging door warmed by the lovely atmosphere and the assumption that there was an actual chef in the kitchen preparing their meals.

I was posted, with no fanfare and little introduction around the kitchen, at the *garde manger* station. Garde manger, which means "keeping to eat" or "keeper of the food," traditionally referred to the cold room in which meats, fish, and other foods that had been preserved were stored, and also to the art of that preservation in forms like charcuterie, terrines, and cheese. It also included using produce creatively. In other words, coping with all the stuff that goes bad if you don't figure out what to do with it in fairly short order, the stuff that in my household gives rise to remarks in front of the open refrigerator along the lines of, "What could we make tonight with beef, heavy cream, kale, mushrooms, and a bunch of radishes? Oh, and also chicken." (One of the skills I hoped to gain at the restaurant, where the chefs stand in the walk-in refrigerator every afternoon in exactly this same way, was how to answer this question with words other than "Um.")

At applewood, garde manger is the station that makes salads and cold appetizers during the dinner service, and it consists of exactly one person. Once things got under way at five o'clock, I would be able to ask questions of anyone I could grab between tasks, theirs and mine, but otherwise I was on my own.

Fortunately, having correctly assumed they wouldn't let me anywhere near the stove on my first day, I'd studied up on my subject the night before. I'd gotten hold of *Garde Manger: The Art and Craft of the Cold Kitchen* (2000), published by the Culinary Institute of America in the Hudson River valley. David and Laura had both gone to cooking school at the CIA—they'd met there, in fact—so I figured its book was a reasonable place to start. I pored over it the night before my first shift and found certain passages popping into my head the next day.

"The opportunities and challenges of the area of cooking known today as garde manger are fascinating," it trumpeted. I couldn't have agreed more. "It is in this specialty that artistic sensibilities can find their outlet." I liked the sound of that. "The quality of the food is still the most important key to success." Check, thanks to applewood's commitment to fresh local products. But then came this. "The visual appearance of the food is a close second. Presenting foods to look their best is a skill that you can spend a lifetime perfecting." Hmm. This must be where the artistic sensibilities came in. But somehow I doubted that David really wanted me to take a lifetime to perfect my salad-plating technique when he had a full book of reservations that night.

I had no chopping skills, I'd never even heard of some of the vinegars I was using, and I had heard of but never seen some of the vegetables (ramps, morels). It hadn't occurred to me to bring my own knives. (When I did the following week, their dullness produced looks of barely suppressed hysteria. Liza, David's other full-time chef, marveled, "It's like they're not even knives!") Apparently there were chefs commuting all over the city with bags of freshly sharpened cutlery—a realization that gave me new perspective on whom to seek out in a crowd during an emergency.

On my list of cold starters that first night were a pea shoot salad with crawfish and brown butter vinaigrette; marinated yellowtail with beets, cilantro, and black bean purée; a cheese plate; and a plate of house-made charcuterie (already prepared, luckily) with garlic crostini. On my to-do list were making the vinaigrette; roasting, peeling, and sectioning the beets; making the black bean purée; and making crostini, which involved cutting loaves of bread into very thin slices, drenching them in garlic-infused olive oil and salt, then baking them in the oven. In other words, a long list of things I had never done before.

But my inexperience didn't seem to faze David, who was used to having externs from cooking school in the kitchen and had once let an art student work garde manger because she wanted to learn about the aesthetics of food. Tall and broad in his chef's jacket, navy-and-white-striped apron and pants, and tortoiseshell Buddy Holly glasses, David thoroughly enjoyed himself in the kitchen and would often ask me, "Did you have fun?" at the end of a night of disasters of varying degrees. He rarely ventured beyond the kitchen during dinner service. Once, when we were discussing the animated movie *Ratatouille*, about a rat named Remy who becomes a chef in a fancy Parisian restaurant, he described the scene he related to most: the one in which the head chef (a human, not a rodent) is summoned to speak to a patron, steps through the swinging door into the dining room, goes bug-eyed with horror at the sight of actual diners, and retreats right back into the kitchen.

David's attitude was, of course, what allowed me to be there at all. In a more typical kitchen filled with tempers and hierarchy, I would never have survived if I'd even been invited in to begin with. But the applewood kitchen didn't run on viciousness or hypercompetitiveness or secrecy; it was the opposite of *Kitchen Confidential*. There was no macho there, not even at the grill, which is traditionally the most macho station (at least according to David, and certainly according to Bill Buford, who wrote memorably about his ferocious, and, it must be said, very macho, efforts to master it during his time in the kitchen at Mario Batali's restaurant Babbo). Instead, the grill at applewood was presided over by a young woman named Sarah. When I asked how she'd ended up working there after a night of "trailing"—standing by and watching the kitchen operate at full tilt to get a sense of the place—she told me, "It was the busiest Saturday night they'd ever had and everyone was calm. It was peaceful, no one was yelling, and the food was beautiful." Or, as the pastry chef put it when I finally got around to working at his station, "When you work for somebody who's already famous, the famous person is not in the kitchen, of course, because they're famous already. Nobody there is your friend because they all want to be famous, too. It's a backstabbing atmosphere."

Laura, small and strong with dark curly hair to her shoulders, was the perfect Harriet to David's Ozzie. The public face of the restaurant, she was charming and social but not soft, and she had a lightning-quick sense of humor. She could read a customer in an instant, and if she saw someone could take it, she was a master of the snappy retort. She was also utterly unapologetic for her tough manner. If you told her teasingly that she was cranky, she played it up, replying with a cranky "So?" When she was in a bad mood, she stormed through the kitchen leaving worried glances in her wake, but she got over it quickly. When she was anxious before dinner service, she barked orders at the servers to clean fingerprints off the glass in the kitchen door or to straighten the napkins on the tables. David was a silent worrier, Laura a loud one; he ran the kitchen and she ran the front of the house, and they never interfered with each other.

What David and Laura had in common (in addition to their marriage and their children, of course) was their understanding of what applewood was. This was something that dated back to 1996 and the first summer after they met in cooking school, when they'd had restaurant jobs at a place in upstate New York called the Old Chatham Sheepherding Company, about a forty-five-minute drive from the Culinary Institute of America.

Old Chatham was then the largest sheep dairy in the

country, with more than two hundred head of sheep. Besides the restaurant, the company included a ten-room inn, a bakery, and a cheesemaking operation. Laura described it for me. "They grew everything for the restaurant but tomatoes and corn. All their own greens, herbs, vegetables. There was a huge greenhouse for starter plants."

Set on six hundred acres of rolling farmland, Old Chatham was, David remembered, "an absolutely beautiful place. In a lot of ways it was like Chez Panisse, but intensified because instead of going out to the farmers they brought all the farmers to them. They had the farm staff, the guy who took care of the sheep, the guy who did the produce."

For David, working at Old Chatham was, in an odd sense, like going home. He grew up in Manhattan's West Village, but a place he refers to simply as "the farm" figures prominently in many conversations with him about food, family, and a lot of other things. A piece of land in Pine Plains, New York, that belongs to the parents of his closest childhood friend, Sean, the farm was where he and Laura and the kids went on their rare days away. It was also where, as a child, he had his first experience of the kind of food he would cook as an adult. "I've been going there all my life. Sean's mom is like my mom," he said. "His little brother was eight years old when his mom had to sit him down and explain to him that I wasn't his brother by blood." The bar David installed at applewood, which Sean's mother had salvaged from a tavern on Twelfth Street in Manhattan, was stored in the cellar at the farm for twenty years until David came calling for it, as if it had been waiting for him all that time.

The job at Old Chatham Sheepherding Company provided David with his first Proustian moment, which came not with a cookie but with a vegetable. "It was tasting the food there," he recalled one day as we were shelling peas, "and realizing I had this vague sort of sense memory of eating tomatoes off the vine up at the farm, munching on them, the dogs running around." Old Chatham reintroduced him to something he'd always known but had buried as he went through chef's training. "At school they teach you that cooking is all these steps and all this secretive stuff and you have to work at it for this long and know all these things, and that's not the case. It just isn't."

For Laura, who grew up in Chicago without a farm to visit, the job at Old Chatham was even more eye-opening. "It changed my ideas about food," she said as I helped her fold napkins for dinner service one afternoon. "Once you pull baby spinach out of the ground and eat it, warmed by the sun, it never tastes as good any other way."

Of course other people already knew this. Out in Berkeley, Chez Panisse had been around for more than twenty years, while in New York City, the Greenmarkets, which had started in 1976 on a single lot, had blossomed into a citywide network of sources for good local food. The Sheas weren't strangers to the idea of local products, either, but those early mornings in the Hudson River valley were the beginning of their real commitment to it. When it came time to choose the suppliers for applewood, those memories were still very much on their minds.

"It's clean food," Laura told me, talking about how they

decided where to buy their food. "Clean local food." In essence, they wanted to re-create, whenever possible, their own experience at Old Chatham—or at least give people the opportunity to have it. It wasn't so much that they insisted everything had to be organic, more that they wanted to know how it was grown and why it was grown that way. Had it been overly processed, or could it be traced back to someone who had put thought into raising it? The guarantee of a person they trusted was worth more than a USDA organic seal or a no-pesticides label. "If you had to choose between an organic product and a local product," Laura explained, "David and I immediately said local. I could call up the farmer, and ask why they treated the Gala apples and what they used. I learned about eco-friendly pesticides from that. You become less closed-minded."

Once, when I was pestering her about defining the restaurant as organic or local or some other term, Laura said, "We wanted to open a place where we could feed everybody the way we feed ourselves and our children." Because I already knew about Sophie and the Cheetos, I pressed her a little further. Where her daughters were concerned, she said, "We're realizing that it's good enough to present good options. That lesson will be learned. They may blow us off and go eat pizza followed by ice cream followed by candy, but they'll know the difference." The same applies to applewood, where the Sheas know they aren't changing the world on a nightly basis, but hope they are at least affecting the way people think about eating. Though they may, in dreamier moments, believe that a single bite of salad has the power to provoke "an epiphany about food and make people not go back to that bag of Dole lettuce," as Laura put it, "we know that's not how it works. We don't advocate for anybody. We're doing what we do within our own framework and not outside of it. I don't really get my face into anyone else's business."

Except, of course, for David's. Restaurants, even small ones like applewood, are complicated organisms. They require constant smart management of a variety of things, which need totally different kinds of attention: food products, bookkeeping, service, and chefs. Every aspect has to be in perfect balance for a meal to go smoothly. For Laura and David, being not only business partners but also married and the parents of two young children complicated matters even more. "Some of the really bad moments for me and Laura are when it's just too much togetherness," David confessed to me once. Their relationship was on display in front of everyone in the restaurant all the time. If Laura was up in the office during prep hours, it was not uncommon to hear her yell "Dave!" in a voice loud enough to echo through the kitchen. This usually resulted in him stopping for a moment, perhaps pulling a face for the rest of us, and yelling back, "In a minute!" He never went to see what she wanted before he finished whatever he was doing, but he always went. If he and Laura were having a disagreement about something unsolvable, he just came back to the kitchen and started cooking again. Even the best-run place has moments of getting through the evening dinner service on sheer guts, and I saw David and Laura bury their argument and do just that more than once.

But I learned all of that later. On my first afternoon at the restaurant, I was far too scared of the food itself to think about where it came from, let alone about the intricacies of David and Laura's marriage. At the garde manger station I faced, in addition to the ingredients for the starters listed on that day's menu, a huge box of morels: damp, dark brown forest mushrooms with narrow stems and honeycombed tops covered with little ridges and pits. The first of the season—it was early May—they had just arrived from Virginia. They would end up in a special appetizer, a "verbal" that wasn't on the written menu, along with veal sweetbreads. David grabbed a few out of the box, split them a bit between finger and thumb, then turned to me and said, in a voice as normal as if he was asking me how I wanted my coffee, "They're filled with worm eggs that are undetectable to the human eye."

The cardboard morel box, which was stained and damp and half-crushed and smelled vaguely like the New Hampshire woods where I hunted for salamanders after summer rainstorms as a child, was sparsely filled at best; this was what eighty dollars worth of fancy mushrooms looked like. And I was supposed to prep them, cut away parts of each one, with some kind of judgment I did not possess. The confidence David either had or was faking in me was unnerving—though I soon learned that one of his great gifts as an employer is divining almost immediately how to use what he has, people and ingredients alike, and then getting the absolute most out of them.

My task was to quarter the morels, except for the ones about the width of my thumb, which I was supposed to leave whole other than trimming a bit of the stem off the bottom. As I took each light, spongy mushroom out of the box, I devised a method of standing them up like little wizened soldiers in a row across my cutting board and stepping back a few paces every now and then to size them up. No doubt I looked as foolish as I felt, but everyone had the grace to go about their business, pretending there was no awkward elephant in a borrowed chef's jacket in the room.

And what a room it was. From the moment I stepped through the glass-paned green door into applewood's kitchen, I felt like Alice down the rabbit hole. Even though it was quite big for a restaurant kitchen (as I learned after arriving and exclaiming "It's so small!" like a true neophyte), it wasn't actually all that big. And it was incredibly full. Below my counter were many jugs holding vinegars (champagne, red wine, white wine, balsamic, sherry, Banyuls), oils, honey, maple syrup, and anything else even remotely saucy. Above it were several dozen quart-sized plastic containers filled with dried fruits, spices, and various nuts. To the left of the counter was wire shelving stretching up toward the high ceiling and stacked perilously with plates, random kitchen utensils, and empty plastic quart containers.

(It would be hard to overemphasize the role of plastic quart containers in the applewood kitchen. Not only was everything from duck innards to blanched peas kept in them, but they served as drinking glasses, too. After a few months of working there, I was constantly reaching for a nonexistent one at home and wondering how I had ever cooked—or quenched my thirst—without them. Somewhere in the back of my mind, I kept trying to work out a way to communicate to the world the profound efficiency of drinking one's morning coffee out of a quart container instead of a ridiculously inadequate mug.)

The door from the dining room swung toward me. "Order in!" called one of the servers. He stuck the top layer of his order ticket into the stainless steel rail above garde manger. It was a table for two (a "two top"), and they wanted a cheese plate and the pea shoot salad to start. Because the pea shoot salad had sautéed crawfish in it, the fish station was in charge of that. That left me with the cheese plate, which I thought I could handle, albeit rather slowly, as it was taking me forever to get the plastic wrap off one of the cheeses.

"You can just cut right through the plastic," David, who was at the fish station, said, swooping over to save me. "Just like this. And then—" he whisked away the piece of wrapping he had sliced off with the neat section of cheese. As he went back to his crawfish, I wondered why it had never occurred to me that I could cut through plastic wrap.

I had many moments like this as I learned about kitchen work. On the day I began by trimming morels, Liza set up my cutting board by soaking paper towels and laying them on the counter, then pressing the board down on top of them. When I looked at her quizzically, she demonstrated the no-slip properties of wet paper towel against stainless steel. Who knew? Several months later, while David was showing me how to make a pork terrine, I discovered that you can bake Saran wrap, and my life has never really been the same since. In the less useful category, I became so accustomed to wiping my hands on my apron or the front of my chef's jacket that I nearly destroyed several sweaters by doing the same thing at home. In a triumph of the banal over the sublime, it was this, rather than my newfound ability to purchase produce with abandon and make a meal from it, that came to mind whenever people asked me whether cooking in a restaurant had changed the way I cooked at home.

But I was happy in the applewood kitchen from the start, squashed in amid the chefs and the shelving and countertops under a ceiling hung with ladles and spoons and strainers and dominated by a huge stainless steel air duct that ran almost the length of the room. The floor was red linoleum, the walls tiled white about three-quarters of the way up, the light fluorescent. The overall effect was overwhelming, but I had left the familiar world behind and I liked having done so. It would be several weeks before I could remember where to find a vegetable peeler or which lowboy refrigerator had the sugar in it. I rarely ventured to the back of the room, which was more or less the domain of the pastry chef, August, though he shared the space with Johnny, who washed pots and pans in a huge double sink at an amazing clip every day starting at three o'clock. Something entirely other was going on back there in pastry, something that involved precise measurements and what looked to be a few actual recipes, two things I had not seen (and never would see) in the part of the kitchen that produced the savory food.

Just beyond the pastry chef's ice cream machine was the door to the office, which was in a loft above the room where Sophie and Tatum had slept every night for the restaurant's first two years. Still painted with scenes of sheep having a tea party, the girls' old haunt was now filled with extra wineglasses and their old futon bed. I tried sometimes to imagine what it would be like to have Jules asleep back there during a long shift, but really, once the controlled frenzy of the dinner service began, it was hard to even remember sometimes that he existed.

Each week the hours flew by while I chopped, diced, and blended. On Thursday the produce arrived in the morning and the meat was delivered in the afternoon—whole goats, pigs, and lambs, and often an enormous hind of veal weighing in the vicinity of a hundred pounds. The animals were stashed in the walk-in to be butchered later, or, if there was not enough meat for dinner service, butchered right then.

When everything was ready, the kitchen door, which remained open in the afternoon, was closed, the lights were dimmed in the dining room, and the candles on the tables and around the room were lit. Depending on how busy the restaurant was, the hours that followed took one of several forms. On a really busy night at applewood, which seats forty-five people at a time (plus six at the bar and another six on the patio in good weather), they'll do a hundred or a hundred and twenty meals ("covers"). Sixty dinners on a weeknight is a decent take, but often they're spread out over the evening in agonizing fashion, four at six o'clock, then nothing until seven-thirty, then a rush at nine and one last gruesome walk-in table at ten-fifteen—"sixty the hard way," in David's parlance. Those were the nights when the chefs did "projects" to keep busy between orders. Sausage got made, rinds and vegetables got pickled, fish got cured.

Those were also the nights when I had time to exercise my artistic sensibilities, time to linger over every plate at garde manger, dressing, garnishing, and organizing each salad and arranging each cheese plate. I didn't know how to make myself useful with brines and meat grinders like the rest of the kitchen staff, but for me every plate was a "project" in itself. It was a little like practicing feng shui on a tiny scale— perhaps the garde manger book was finally having an effect on me—and I was getting into the aesthetics of "presenting foods to look their best." Lettuce leaves went into the bowl with the spine down, ruffled edges turned up so they were open to diners. Cheese wedges, placed next to the accompanying stack of garlic crostini, always had the uncovered end pointing toward the edge of the plate, an invitation to cut in. When it came to the arrangement of the wedges and crostini, though, there was room for individuality. No two of us did it quite the same way—in the fluidity of such a small kitchen, even though everyone had an official station, no one was above stepping over and helping out if needed— and David, as much as his standards were impeccable and his sense of hospitality enormous, liked it that way.

Once when David was training a new chef, I asked what he planned to tell him. "Cook for yourself," he answered.

"Whatever anybody has to say shouldn't impact you all that much. If you're trying, if you care, that's enough." He paused, then added, "I'm going to say, 'Just pretend you're at home cooking for you and your wife.'" Then he tied on his apron and headed for the grill.

And though of course this was not the whole story and the new chef didn't last the week because, however he cooked for his wife, it was not the way he needed to cook at apple-wood, I knew David's sentiment was genuine. After all, there are ideals and reality in everything.

2

❖

We Eat What We Are

MY FIRST WORD, uttered sometime in the winter of 1971–72, was "cookie." Naturally, I leapt at the chance to spend half my week in a kitchen where a steady supply of baked goods was handed around at all hours. It will not, perhaps, surprise you to learn that my nickname as a young child was "Miss Carbohydrate," nor that my belly was extraordinarily large (though, thankfully, it disappeared right around the age when having a midsection shaped like a bowling ball is no longer considered adorable). My sister, who was four and a half when I was born and a keen observer of the world, called me Mush. Now that she's a mother (of two children who, annoyingly, will eat anything she puts in front of them), I have been promoted to Auntie Mush.

There is, of course, nothing like having a child of your own to make your family suddenly recall all the quirks and characteristics of your childhood. And so, soon after I had Jules—whose first word, you may also not be surprised to learn, was "no!" followed almost immediately by "this!" so that he could tell us about all the food items that utterly repulsed him and then about the very few that didn't—there were many reminiscences about what a ham I had been, and how I had my first haircut at six months, and also, yes, what a dreadfully picky eater I was.

Among other things, I refused to eat sauce of any kind until I was into the double digits. I even hated stopping at McDonald's on family trips because in those days they served nothing but burgers and it was impossible to get one without mustard and ketchup already on it (I guess I was ahead of Eric Schlosser in judging fast food, though for all the wrong reasons). I can remember pouting in the backseat of the car as everyone else munched away, pretending to be interested in the scenery along the New York State Thruway or the New Jersey Turnpike as I plotted world domination and the plain hamburgers that would be served across the globe once I was in charge.

Given all of this, my time at applewood was tinged with the reckless abandon of a woman running from her past, which had, as the past always does, returned to haunt me in the eating habits of my son. I couldn't help feeling it was at least partially my fault that, unintentionally, Jules was foiling one of my most basic instincts. Every time he refused his dinner (or his breakfast or his lunch), I thought of M. F. K. Fisher, who wrote that "one of the pleasantest of all emotions is to know that I, I with my brain and my hands, have nourished my beloved few, that I have concocted a stew or a story, a rarity or a plain dish, to sustain them truly against the hungers of the world." The stories I had down, but I wanted the stew, too. So, unable to please my son, I settled for feeding strangers at the restaurant.

The first physical manifestation of this zeal appeared on my hands: by midsummer I had almost no fingernails left, and I had discovered that it's possible to do a great many things without them. If you're an amateur chef, it's also probably wise to buy stock in a bandage company. Adhesive can cover a multitude of sins, including the absence of a sizeable chunk of thumbnail and the thumb that was once beneath it, an injury caused by repeated idiotic use of a mandoline. Or, as someone muttered when Liza was putting it together for me to use on the last day I had a thumbnail for many months, "the most dangerous tool in the kitchen."

It was also, according to Liza, a tool that "makes everything so easy!" (Oh, to have a dollar for every time I proved her wrong on that count.) Liza, who had never bothered to go to cooking school, was a born chef. As children, she and her brother had run a little café at home, cooking for their parents on anniversaries and birthdays. "I always made up my own recipes," she mused, mincing chives. "I've always been somebody who goes to the grocery store, sees what's there, and makes something up as I'm shopping. I read cookbooks and take them in, and then I make other things."

I listened to Liza with great interest and a bit of envy, as this was, in fact, exactly the kind of person I'd always wanted to be.

Little by little, Liza and David were trying to point me in that direction, and like her boss, Liza displayed a charmingly misplaced level of confidence in me—laughable knives notwithstanding. One day in June she asked me to make a jicama slaw. This required first peeling the fibrous, papery skin off of the jicama root, which was the shape of a slightly squashed sphere, to uncover the crisp white flesh with a consistency similar to a raw potato. Then you used the mandoline to slice the jicama, then you julienned it and added it to citrus-marinated cipollini onions (also sliced on the mandoline) and minced jalapeño. It seemed like an awful lot of slicing, but Liza demonstrated enthusiastically, knocking out a series of perfect jicama slices, her arm moving back and forth in a steady rhythm. Buoyed by her positive attitude, I plunged in with gusto.

Roughly five seconds later I had, instead of neat slices, jicama gone haywire. There were little chunks and pieces all over my cutting board, not a perfect slice to be found anywhere. I kept trying, and was rewarded about two minutes later when I grated right through my plastic glove and into the thumbnail of my right hand, which was clutching the jicama in a claw-like fashion. Soon after that, because there was nothing else left to mangle, I sliced into the skin of my thumb, which began to bleed a little bit inside my replacement glove, now also cut open. I bandaged it up and persisted without stopping to ask anyone what I was doing wrong—I was worried about losing face, and I'm nothing if not hard-headed; like mother, like son. Over and over, just when I thought I'd cut as deeply into my flesh as was possible, I managed to slice off just one more millimeter (and through one more glove), leaving my thumb a tingling, smarting mess, though at least these later slices were too superficial to bleed. I continued until I had sliced enough jicama to ensure that everyone who ordered the diver scallops it was to be served with could have a portion. Then I put my first imperfect jicama hunks and lumps into a bowl from which everyone in the kitchen could help themselves while they worked.

Still, I was relaxed in spite of the pain (I'll say just one more thing: jalapeño juice in fresh open wounds). It was the longest day of the year, the summer solstice, as I merrily went about the destruction of my thumb. The walk-in refrigerator downstairs was so crammed with produce that no one could actually walk in. The huge number of boxes and crates taking up most of the floor space had forced me to balance on one foot when I put away duck breasts earlier that day. There were carrots as fat as my wrist, fava beans in their long, dingy pale green pods, the last of the English peas, four kinds of lettuce (one fantastically named Red Cross), arugula, sunchokes, hot banana peppers, bok choy, spinach, basil, morels, and fresh chives capped with purple flowers, which gave off a delicious oniony smell and became garnish for a soup that night.

All of it had come from nearby farms, most of them in upstate New York, in the Delaware River valley and Columbia County. There was nothing in there I wouldn't have gobbled up in a heartbeat, though possibly this ecstatic feeling was as much the result of the forty-degree temperature of the walk-in as it was a reaction to the fruits and vegetables.

Outside the restaurant, it was eighty-five degrees and ninety percent humidity. In the kitchen, which I once heard David describe as "one of those kitchens that's really hot in the summer and really cold in the winter," it was unquantifiably worse. The kind of worse that produces steady rivulets of sweat running down your chest under the two layers of your shirt and chef's jacket that don't let up for the entire duration of a ten-hour dinner shift.

But the heat was nothing compared to what was happening at home. During the month of June, Jules cried at dinner every single night, or at least this was the only thing I could bring myself to write down about the month other than that he was living almost exclusively on yogurt and bananas, with some nuts and crackers thrown in. I, who had shunned books about pregnancy, childbirth, decorating your nursery, and most other baby-related topics (except for that one about sleep, for obvious reasons), had finally given in and begun reading about how to get a child to eat. I hoped to discover a magic solution that I could implement in some specified number of easy steps. Being in the restaurant kitchen, with its utterly logical—if occasionally dangerous—processes of slicing, dicing, blanching, and puréeing, had made me even more aware of how much I loved having a plan. There were no recipes at applewood, but there were universally applicable methods for getting things done. You prepped, cooked, plated, and sent out to the dining room, and before long the plate came back empty and you knew someone on the other side of the swinging door was happy.

All of which was much more satisfying than reading books about stubborn toddlers and their wretched eating habits, let alone actually coping with one of these children. In the books I found sentences like this one, which confirmed yet again that Jules was not even an ordinary picky eater: "When the toddler goes through the long warm-up of twenty meals to learn to eat a vegetable, you won't worry if you understand that this is all part of the learning process." Well, the book was right, I wouldn't have worried at all about that. But with Jules the widely touted theory that children need ten, fifteen, even twenty exposures to a new food before they'll eat it did not apply. Not one little bit. There was no getting him to try anything no matter how many times we exposed him to it. If we suggested he taste it, he ignored us. If we said nothing, trying to "be appropriately unconcerned" as one expert suggested, he ignored the food. As his vocabulary expanded, he began to look at things on his plate and say, for example, "No chicken. No pasta. No fish." He knew what everything was, and he knew he didn't want it.

At last I turned once again to M. F. K. Fisher. I needed a book about the human relationship to food rather than one about how to induce your offspring to eat—emotion rather than psychology—and Fisher's work fit the bill perfectly. "When a man is small, he loves and hates food with a ferocity which soon dims . . . ," she wrote in *Serve It Forth*

(1937). "His throat will close, and spots of nausea and rage swim in his vision." It occurred to me as I took this in that perhaps, through some feat of reincarnation, Fisher had met my son. "It is hard, later, to remember why, but at the time there is no pose in his disgust. He cannot eat; he says, 'To hell with it!'"

Now this was what I was looking for, because all around me, parents were telling stories about their children eating exotic food. Children who loved sushi (Jules wouldn't even try rice) or eggplant, or something else improbable and charming. One night Sophie and Tatum came into the restaurant with their babysitter and word came back to the kitchen that Sophie wanted duck. A few minutes after the plate went out, it was returned with an apology—she had meant to ask for duck confit.

Several days later, utterly despairing, I flung myself down on a chair near Laura while she got changed for dinner service and asked her how on earth she had produced two children who ate duck confit.

This was the moment when I realized that if David was an overt softie, Laura was a secret one. Beneath all her wise-cracking—and not even very far beneath it—was something entirely different. I would never have guessed it, but later on, during a slow period in the kitchen when David and I were talking about our children, he told me that Laura refused to talk to Sophie and Tatum on the phone when they were apart because she couldn't bear to hear them upset. I also discovered that she was the engineer of all sorts of romantic escapades on behalf of customers, like incorporating marriage proposals into the dessert menu and offering glasses of champagne when these proposals were accepted. (Reverting to her tougher persona, she would come back to the kitchen and side with the groom if she felt the bride-to-be had not answered as effusively as she should have.)

But none of this was known to me that day I begged her for her secret, and I expected that my misery might inspire one of her snappy, funny remarks. Instead, I got nothing but sympathy. "For the first four years, Sophie ate anything," Laura recalled. "People said it was because David and I are chefs. I started to think maybe there was something to that, maybe the way we feel about food had an effect."

I was about to protest that Noah and I feel great about food, too—we love food! Then she continued. "But then at four, one by one, there were fewer and fewer foods she would eat. Now it's chicken."

The idea of a Shea child refusing to eat chicken cheered me right up. It also reminded me of something else I had read in a book about feeding children. "Parents of finicky preschoolers almost always tell me the same story," the author had written. "'She ate well when she was just starting out on solid foods, but then when she was a toddler she would only eat certain foods. Now she won't even eat what she did when she was a toddler.'" Then the author had delivered a damning judgment: "In that phrase describing the toddler, 'she would only eat certain foods,' the parent is telling me that she was catered to."

Upon reading this, I had questioned whether Noah and I had been indulging Jules's fondness for yogurt and bananas just because we wanted him to eat something, as of course we did. It's very hard to ponder sending your one-year-old to bed hungry. But knowing Laura, I seriously doubted that she had catered to Sophie, so maybe we were in the clear. I was about to ask what she thought about this when she shrugged and said, "They're people, and sometimes it's a political protest and sometimes they really don't like it."

I expect to see Jules on some kind of picket line by the time he's five.

❖

"When people enter the kitchen," the novelist Laurie Colwin wrote in her wonderful book of food essays *Home Cooking*, "they often drag their childhood in with them." I had thought I was coming to the kitchen to escape the one aspect of Jules's childhood that was driving me absolutely crazy. Instead, I stumbled across my own early years and found a small, unexpected salvation there.

One of the most cherished activities of my youth was making forays with my father to the Cellar at Macy's, a gourmet mecca of a kind that is now commonplace in cities like New York but was still exotic back then, especially to a young child. There, we would buy two things I loved dearly: freshly baked "salt sticks," stubby, narrow rolls covered with rock salt and caraway seeds; and candied orange peel. Both these treats evoked for my father memories of his own childhood in Czechoslovakia, and we would often talk about his favorite sweets and cakes that couldn't be bought in America. As we stood on one of Macy's rattling old wooden escalators one afternoon, a dreamy look came across his face as he described a striped coconut confection. I must have been about six years old, and it was the first time I really understood that he had had a life before my mother, my sister, and me, in a place very far away that he had not been back to for many years. On the bus ride home, while I tried to imagine him as a little boy in middle-European short pants and knee socks, we demolished our spoils, arriving at our apartment far too stuffed for lunch.

I hadn't thought about those trips to the Cellar for a very long time until one day in the kitchen at applewood. I had just finished peeling an enormous metal sheet tray of roasted cipollini onions, which were mixed into many of the vegetables for extra flavor before plating a dish to be served, and was looking to take a little break before moving on to a similarly huge tray of roasted beets. I stepped over to the grill, where Sarah was scribbling ideas for the evening's meat dishes on a paper towel. Sweetbreads with turnips, apple-ginger compote, and brown butter; crispy pork belly with grilled potatoes and scallion purée; roasted rabbit with fingerling potatoes, rapini, and basil pesto; grilled goat with cannellini beans and squash; duck breast with red cabbage and candied orange peel.

The last item on Sarah's list caught my eye. Candied orange peel. If she had written it on the paper towel, that must mean she knew how to make it. And if Sarah knew how to make candied orange peel, chances were there was some in the vicinity. Then I saw it—a full plastic quart container sitting on her stainless steel counter. It was as though I'd stumbled right back into the Cellar at Macy's, only this time I wasn't separated from the bounty by a glass case. I dipped a spoon in to swipe a few pieces. Savoring the citrusy sweetness, I asked Sarah how she made it, thinking that if I gained the power to produce my own candied orange peel I would have penetrated one of the great secrets of, if not *the* universe, at least my universe.

"It's *so* easy," she said, characteristically encouraging me as she caramelized shallots for a chanterelle mushroom ragout with polenta. (The grill station also made the nightly vegetarian entrée, an extra task that nearly pushed me over the edge every time I worked it.) I watched intently as she pantomimed julienning orange peel. "Then you toss it in a pot of water, boil it, change the water, boil it and change the water three more times, add the sugar the last time and then let it reduce until all the liquid is gone," she said. "Voilà!" Okay, how hard could it be, I thought, heading back to my beets. I craved that orange peel, and since Sarah needed hers for the duck I didn't think she was going to let me make off with the whole quart.

At that time I was especially prone to the kind of longing triggered by the candied orange peel, because my father, he of the giggling on escalators and the unfettered joy in eating candy before lunch, had died when Jules was four months old. It had been left to me to pass on to my son all of the details that made him whole, eccentric snacking habits included.

It had not occurred to me that I would find anything at applewood to remind me of my father (another reason, perhaps, for my flight from my regular life into the restaurant's kitchen). Despite his love of good food, he was a man blissfully free of the ability to cook much of anything beyond a very festive cheese fondue. But of course there's a good deal more to food than cooking, as I had discovered on that escalator.

And so it was with more than just normal apprehension that I bought half a dozen oranges (yes, they were completely out of season) and carried them home one evening to attempt Sarah's recipe. As I stood over my stove watching the matchsticks of peel churning around in the boiling water, I thought of my father and all the times we'd eaten it together, often to the point of gleeful illness, in cities and towns around the world. My heart pounded at the idea of being able to recreate, in some small way, the food that strung those many memories together. When the final pan of water had evaporated, leaving just the peel, now coated in sugar, I put a piece on my tongue and tasted those long-ago afternoons.

Jules, who had learned to walk by this time, was using his new talent to get as close to the hot stove as possible. In spite of his eating habits, he was usually good for something sweet, so I gave him a piece to try.

"Like it!" he exclaimed in a surprised voice, chewing and raising his bright blue eyes up to mine. "More!"

And suddenly my father was there, if only for an instant,

visible in the look of sheer delight on Jules's face. A few lines of a poem by Wyatt Prunty that I'd loved for many years, since long before I had any acquaintance with any of its subject matter, rushed into my mind. He was talking about the arrival of his own son, but he could have been standing in my dining room watching Jules munch orange peel when he wrote:

> . . . your birth was my close land
> Turned green, the stone rolled back for leaving,
> My father dead and you returned.

My own father, I saw all at once, was not lost to Jules after all, and not quite as lost to me as I had thought.

❖ Candied Orange Peel

6 oranges
1 cup sugar

1. Remove the peel from the oranges by cutting off each end, then cutting from top to bottom of the orange, following the shape of the fruit, so the peel comes off in big sections. Do not cut off the white pith, just the peel.

2. Julienne the peel into thin strips.

3. Place the peel in cold water in a pot and bring to a boil to remove bitterness. Repeat 3 times, changing the water each time.

4. Place drained peel in a pot with cold water and sugar, bring to a boil, and reduce it until all the liquid is gone.

5. Feed to your toddler against the bad advice of everyone who says it will ruin his teeth. Do not feel guilty.

Serves about 24 as garnish, or 1 as a source of immense happiness.

❖ Jicama Slaw

10–12 cipollini onions
fresh-squeezed juice of 4–5 oranges, adjusted for taste
fresh-squeezed juice of 4 limes
fresh-squeezed juice of 4 lemons
1 large or 2 small jicama roots (about 2 pounds)
zest of 1 large lemon
zest of 2–3 limes
⅓ cup olive oil
salt
3 jalapeños, seeds removed

1. Peel the cipollinis and use a mandoline to slice them very thinly. Set the slices to marinate in a bowl of mixed citrus juices, amounting to about one-third of the total juice, made up of 2 parts orange juice to 1½ parts lime juice to 1 part lemon juice.

2. Peel the jicama root and slice it about ⅛ inch thick on the mandoline.

3. Cut the jicama slices into matchsticks.

4. In a large bowl, mix the jicama with the lemon and lime zest, then add the remaining juices in the same ratio used for marinating the cipollinis.

5. Add olive oil and salt to taste.

6. Slice the jalapeños about ⅛ inch thick on the mandoline, then mince them and add to the mixture.

7. Add the marinated cipollinis and, if necessary, some of the liquid they were in.

Serves 4 as a starter or a side.

3

❖

What Is Cheese?

By the time I had been at applewood for a few months, I had settled into the weekly schedule. The restaurant served dinner Tuesdays through Saturdays, brunch on Sundays, and was closed Mondays. Tuesday morning was when the kitchen came back to life, when the chefs went down to the walk-in and pondered its contents most intently because they knew they wouldn't get anything new to play with until Thursday. There was a pleasant rhythm to this cycle—the depleting of resources in the early part of the week followed by the bounty of Thursday morning deliveries and the excitement of a new set of vegetables and meats to experiment with. (David once told me that he actually dreamed about recipes.) This regularity was punctuated now and then by the cheese deliveries.

Unlike everything else, cheese arrived at random and, to my surprise, usually by UPS. I discovered this one day while I was working at garde manger, slicing beets and making vinaigrettes. An ordinary brown box appeared on the stainless steel counter and I looked up just in time to see the UPS guy disappearing through the swinging door. The box could have contained almost anything—books, shoes, DVDs, toothbrushes—but instead, the first slice of the knife into the packing tape released the unmistakably pungent odor of cheese. Inside was an ashy gray wheel, which I took down to the walk-in, my mind spinning.

You can mail cheese, I thought. *Wait until I tell my friends about this.*

It had never occurred to me that sitting in the very same UPS truck as all those Amazon packages and shipments of diapers was something so delectable. Who had packed the box and where? I associated UPS with offices and Xerox machines, not fields and farms.

A lot of the cheese brought by UPS came from a small dairy farm in the middle of Connecticut called Cato Corner. It was only about a hundred and twenty miles away, and I thought it would be an ideal place to start learning more about who, and what, was behind applewood's food.

On a sunny Wednesday in June, I got in my car and drove north. A small herd of caramel-colored Jersey cows munching grass behind a wooden fence was the first sign that I'd reached my destination. The cows were an anomaly amid the modest, essentially suburban houses set close to the winding road. They appeared all of a sudden, the long red barn behind them set off by tiers of rolling green pasture that seemed to rise up to the clouds.

When I stepped out of the car onto a dirt and gravel driveway, a rush of wind in the surrounding trees filled my ears. It was an unblemished summer day, one of the kind the poet Philip Larkin described as "emblems of perfect happiness," made all the more perfect by the fact that I seemed to have stepped into a page from Jules's Old MacDonald book. I could hear cows lowing and dogs barking as I walked toward a small gray shed next to the barn. The strong but not unpleasant scent of manure and hay and farm animals filled the air. A black and white rooster scrabbled past, and I watched it hurry to an aging white farmhouse surrounded by trees.

Entering the shed, I found two women dressed in tall white galoshes, big white plastic aprons, and shower caps that looked to be made of cheesecloth—a very Willy Wonka effect. Cheryl was the first to introduce herself. A former chef who had tired of the taxing hours of restaurant work, she now made cheese at the farm full time. Helping her that day was Dianna, who was an accountant in Manhattan three days a week and spent one day every week making cheese as an antidote to the commuting and the rat race. For now, one day was all the time she could spare, but she was hoping to get out of accounting and onto the farm full time. As the women wrapped pieces of cheese in wax paper (no doubt they had packed at least some of those UPS boxes), Cheryl told me they sold about five hundred pounds of cheese per weekend at the New York City Greenmarkets. Recently, local people had started to buy their cheese, too. When I asked why, she gestured to a poster taped to the door. On it were a photo of a farm stand and the words "Homeland security. Buy local. It matters." "People want to know where their food is from after the whole spinach scare," she explained.

It had been almost a year since the first death from *E. coli*–tainted spinach grown in California—two more people later died, and more than two hundred others got sick—but the episode was still very much on people's minds, not least because it was followed fairly quickly by another *E. coli* outbreak linked to green onions. (Since then there have been a number of other major food recalls in quick succession, including everything from peanuts and peanut butter to cookie dough to beef in 2009 alone.) That spinach had come from large, commercial produce farms, some organic, some not, and was eventually found to have been contaminated by manure from nearby cattle, probably delivered through groundwater. The growers had not been at fault, but it had taken almost a month for health officials to reach that conclusion. In the meantime, people had plenty of time to reflect on the fact that they didn't know much about who was growing their food or how.

Hence the increased sales at Cato Corner, a place small enough to maintain almost total control over land, animals, and product. As the farm staff is happy to tell anyone who asks, they adhere to strict inspection and hygiene practices that far exceed what's required by the FDA and the Connecticut Department of Agriculture, testing all of their milk immediately for listeria, a big threat in dairy production, and periodically for all kinds of other bacteria. They use anti-biotics only in the event of illness and never inject their cows with hormones to make them produce more milk, a common practice at big commercial dairies. They want their animals to be healthy so they produce the best milk—not the most milk—possible, and they want their land to be healthy so it helps feed the animals, all of which results in delicious, worry-free cheese. Even though the FDA treats raw milk like a toxic substance, banning interstate sales and requiring cheese made from it to be aged at least sixty days before being sold, if the milk comes from a place like Cato Corner it's a pretty safe bet.

As Cheryl and Dianna were explaining some of this to me, Mark Gillman, the resident cheesemaker, emerged from the cheesemaking room behind the shop, his curly red hair and beard encased in shower caps. "Oh!" he said. "I forgot you were coming."

Mark grew up on the farm, which is owned by his mother, Elizabeth MacAlister. Wiry and energetic, he looked as if he had just come from another world, and once I got into the cheesemaking room myself, I could see that he had—a world that resembled a fetid New York City street on a hot, humid summer afternoon.

Outside the cheesemaking room, all was green and fresh. Inside it, the air was about ninety degrees and smelled totally rancid. Walking into it was like getting inside someone's dirty sneaker—or someone's carton of spoiled milk. I had scrubbed myself with sanitizing fluid, washing up to my elbows like a surgeon (in that environment, Mark said, "stuff is growing, and you want it to be the right stuff"), then rinsed off and donned the green Wellies I had brought with me, plus a shower cap, plastic gloves, and one of the farm's huge white aprons, which hung almost to my ankles. The door was sealed behind us to keep out the "bad" bacteria: cheese is created by encouraging and then controlling the growth of the specific bacteria you want for each variety.

The room was dominated by an oval stainless steel cheese bath about three feet deep and ten feet long, filled with twenty-seven hundred pounds of milk that had been warmed to ninety degrees (most cheeses are made with milk warmed to a temperature between eighty-eight and ninety-two degrees). For every round of cheesemaking, Cato Corner uses the milk from one day's milking of about thirty cows. Besides the cheese bath there were two long, narrow stainless steel sinks and a stainless steel cheese press, which we didn't use that day since we were making an uncooked, unpressed soft cheese. (Cooking and pressing both get rid of a lot of moisture, which results in hard cheeses like cheddar or Gouda.) A small window above the sinks looked directly into the cow barn, while another offered a view of the grass at the front of the property where the cows had been grazing when I arrived.

The cheese we were making that day was called Hooligan, a soft, washed-rind variety like Munster or Taleggio. "It's a stinky cheese so it seemed like it deserved an appropriately troublemaker sort of name," said Mark. The twenty-seven hundred pounds of milk (almost three hundred fourteen gallons) would make about two hundred one-pound wheels. Mark had already added the starter culture, dried bacteria that speeds up the transformation of lactose into lactic acid, the first step in turning milk into cheese, and also plays a role in the breakdown of milk proteins so that the cheese develops flavor as it ages: older cheese is sharper because the proteins have broken down more. Mark orders his various cultures freeze-dried from a European provider in Canada. "It's basically a commercial starter culture that's created by isolating the bacteria from some of the best cheese in Europe," he said. Because Cato Corner's cows graze from May through November on the tiers of pasture I had seen rising up behind the barn, and because Mark uses their milk raw, he uses much less starter culture than someone working with pasteurized milk would need. Pasteurization kills the milk's natural bacteria and also makes many of its enzymes inactive, and since these two elements contribute enormously to the development of flavor as cheese ages, their absence means more starter culture has to be introduced to compensate.

At last I had the answer to one of my main questions about raw milk cheese: Why does it taste so much better than cheese made from pasteurized milk? Because it's naturally complicated: it tastes like the bacteria produced by grasses, flowers, weeds, and all the other things cows eat when they roam the landscape. "There are millions of micro-organisms in all that," Mark told me. "Any commercial starter culture has fairly limited strains. We've got millions of bacteria from the grass and weeds that are just naturally occurring." When he said this, I thought of the novelist Italo Calvino, who wrote, "Behind every cheese there is a pasture of a different green under a different sky."

As for my other big question about raw milk cheese—one that was on the mind of the FDA and of every pregnant woman whose doctor had warned her not to go near any soft cheese, which seems to function as an incorrect equivalency for unpasteurized cheese—Mark put it to rest, at least for me, with a simple statement. When I asked him about the risks of eating cheese made from raw milk, he said, "We have two little kids. The first pregnancy my wife ate no raw milk cheese. The second time she ate a lot of it."

We went back to the Hooligan at hand. In addition to the starter culture, Mark had added rennet, the stomach enzyme that enables calves to digest milk. Rennet, obtained from animals that are being slaughtered for other reasons, usually for food, coagulates the milk and together with the starter culture helps break down proteins to determine texture and taste. Once the milk has firmed up, it can be cut into curds, which are the solids that get turned into cheese. While many cheesemakers have switched to cheaper, genetically engineered vegetable rennets in place of the traditional calf rennet, Cato Corner has not. "People who are squeamish about animal products may not like it," Mark told me, "but in my mind it's a way to use all of an animal that's being harvested anyway. And it's a natural product."

I got into the cheese room about forty minutes after Mark had added the rennet, and the milk had already taken on the consistency of yogurt. He stuck a big blade into the bath to check for firmness. "The flavor of any cheese comes from the breakdown of fat and protein in the aging process," he explained. "Each cheese is a little bit different in terms of what you want to happen. Feta, you develop a lot of acidity very quickly and you end up with the crumbly feta texture. Swiss, you develop your acidity fairly slowly and its pH stays high, and it has low acid. That leaves it very high in calcium, which makes it chewier."

Essentially, cheesemaking is the management of four basic ingredients: milk, starter culture, rennet, and time. Various amounts and combinations of these key elements yield different cheeses, with the flavor of the raw milk playing the wild card according to the season. "The milk is always changing," Mark said as he wiped the knife clean and hung it back on a peg on the wall. Richer milk, for example, winter milk—from the months when the cows eat local hay and grain rather than grass—needs more culture and less rennet because it has more protein. In order to produce more or less consistent cheese over the span of seasons (though no two batches of artisanal cheese will ever be exactly the same), according to Mark, "you want the rate of acidification to proceed at roughly the same rate in February as in June. Ninety percent of the work of an aged cheese takes place in the first six hours."

Part of that work was cutting the curds in the cheese bath, which had solidified into a firm, gelatin-like consistency while we were talking. Mark ran a curd knife, a rectangular wire-strung paddle with a long handle, first horizontally and then vertically through the quivering yellowish-white mass, separating it into neat little cubes that immediately began to collapse as the whey—the liquid by-product of curdled milk—leaked out of them. While he worked, my mind drifted back to those UPS boxes that arrived at the restaurant.

One of the cheeses that came frequently was Cato Corner's dry, nutty, crystal-filled hard cheese called Bloomsday, and I had become addicted to it on garde manger. As Mark and I bent over the bath with Cheryl and Dianna, turning the piles of curds with our plastic-gloved hands over and over again until they were more glob-like than cubed and most of the whey had seeped out and been pumped into a vat for the cows to drink—and made many truly terrible jokes, starting with the perfect name for a new soap opera, "As the Curd Turns"—I had Bloomsday on the brain. By the time we loaded the curds into small plastic molds that looked like miniature laundry baskets and set them on a sanitized wooden plank over the sink to finish draining, I was hankering for a fix.

Either Mark could sense this or he was just hungry. As we emerged from the cheesemaking room he suggested we go across to the farmhouse for some lunch.

There, at a table covered by a cloth printed with cows and the slogan "Contented Cows Give Sweet Milk," in a room featuring peeling radish-print wallpaper and a small bookshelf holding, among other reading material, *2000 Spanish Verbs*, *Milk Them for All Their Worth*, and *The New Agrarianism*, we ate one of Cato Corner's blue cheeses, Black Ledge Blue, plus an unbelievable amount of Bloomsday. As we each bit into our third Bloomsday sandwich Mark looked up at me, wild-eyed for a second, and said, "I love this cheese!"

It turned out that my new favorite cheese (and Mark's apparently, at least that day) was a mistake Mark had made one year on June 16, also known as Bloomsday because it's the day on which James Joyce's *Ulysses,* the story of twenty-four hours in the life of a man named Leopold Bloom, takes place. Taped up next to the Homeland Security poster in the cheese shed was a passage from the book that seemed to say, in simple terms (not usually Joyce's strong suit), everything I was finding to be true during my days at the restaurant:

> —How much sir? asked the old woman.
> —A quart, Stephen said.
> He watched her pour into the measure and thence into the jug rich white milk . . . She praised the goodness of the milk, pouring it out. Crouching by a patient cow at daybreak in the lush field, a witch on her toadstool, her wrinkled fingers quick at the squirting dugs. They lowed about her whom they knew, dew-silky cattle . . .
> —It is indeed, ma'am, Buck Mulligan said, pouring milk into their cups.
> —Taste it, sir, she said.
> He drank at her bidding.
> If we could live on good food like that, he said to her somewhat loudly, we wouldn't have the country full of rotten teeth and rotten guts. Living in a bogswamp, eating cheap food and the streets paved with dust, horsedung and consumptives' spits.

Mark had come home to cheesemaking at Cato Corner after teaching English in Baltimore's inner city for a decade.

When he was growing up, his parents had raised sheep and goats for meat and wool. "It was not a self-supporting farm," he recalled. "My parents both worked off the farm, too. We worked after school and we had about a hundred ewes and forty goats." I had to laugh as the animal laundry list went on. "We raised three pigs, somewhere in there they had a cow or two. It was a time-consuming hobby." Mark decided to return partly because his mother, Elizabeth, had begun to change the land back into the dairy farm it had been when she bought it in 1979, which would turn it from a hobby into a self-sustaining business. "She started by getting a loan and putting in all the equipment," Mark said. "I was teaching and thought I'd come home and check it out for a while." That was it for him. "I love it," he told me, as though it wasn't obvious to anyone who saw him at work. "It's hard to imagine doing something else at this point."

After lunch Mark asked, rather jauntily, "Do you want to go flip Hooligans?" We scrubbed down again and went back to the cheese room where, in the forty minutes or so that had elapsed while we were eating, the curds in their little baskets had already bonded together enough that each proto-cheese could be dumped out of its mold, damp and gelatinous in the palm of my hand, and flipped over on its way to being dumped back in. They would sit on the plank, with a few more flips, until all the whey had drained out. Then Mark would take them to ripen in the cheese cave built under the shed—"We have lots of naturally occurring molds down there that are going to help contribute to the flavor. I'm not even exactly sure how they work," he confessed. He would bathe them in salt brine twice a week for eight weeks until their rinds were a deep orange color and sticky to the touch. When I asked him how he knew for sure when they were ripe, he laughed. "I taste 'em!"

I went down to the cave with him to check on the progress of some older Hooligans, where I discovered a kind of library, with cheeses in place of books. The floor was concrete, and the cave was kept at a chilly fifty degrees and a very damp eighty-five to ninety percent humidity. The stench of cheese in varying stages of bacterial growth made inhaling almost painful. As far as the eye could see were cheeses stacked on open wooden shelves, hundreds of them of all sizes. Each shelf was labeled with the date the cheese sitting on it had been made. The newest group of Hooligans looked almost like cakes, yellow with pink edges, as they moldered on their dark shelf. As the dates went further back, the cheeses turned to various shades of orange, then that sticky deep orange, with all the rawness and newness gone. When Mark mentioned that they smelled like body odor because they were made with some of the same bacteria that grows on the human body, I decided it was time to get away from the cheese and into the open air.

Outside again, I met up with Elizabeth for a tour of the barn. Thanks to her mix of Scottish, Irish, and Welsh ancestry, most of the cows had names like Moira and Deirdre and Maeve, but there were a few standouts called Juanita, Doozie, and my personal favorite, Gin. Elizabeth, who had long gray hair and an infectious laugh, got up at two-thirty every morning to tend to them. As I watched her greeting them and thumping their sides, I suddenly felt like an absolute brat for ever mentioning sleep deprivation when Jules was a newborn.

Thirty-two cows were "milkers" that day. (Cows lactate for about ten months of the year, and only after they've had a calf, an event delightfully named "freshening," hardly the word I would have used to describe myself after giving birth.) When we walked in they were being milked three at a time by machine, their udders hooked up to vacuum pumps that combined all their milk in a stainless steel tank. The ones who weren't on deck were milling around in an open area, chewing their cud. Some of them were more tan than caramel, some a darker brown. Several had heart-shaped splotches of white above and between their eyes.

Some of the animals, Elizabeth explained, weren't particularly "good specimens" by cattle-breeders' standards. Their bodies weren't lined up properly or they just didn't look quite right. Unable to bear the thought of their being punished for their imperfections, she had either adopted or bought them from the farms where they weren't wanted. Looking into their eyes, I could see why. The awkward bulk of their bodies seemed to disappear behind the calm brown depths.

We left the barn and walked up through the pastures, accompanied by Harp and Flute, the farm's border collies. This was where the cows grazed on forty-two acres in twelve-hour rotations to keep the land fertile and the milk delicious.

In every bite of Bloomsday, I was tasting these fields, planted mostly with wild clover and bluegrass. But the cows ate almost anything they could find, Elizabeth said as we walked, the dogs bounding around us and barking enthusiastically. "The one thing they won't eat is thistle," she mentioned as we passed some purple blooms.

As we ascended the fields, she told me the pastures had just been approved for inclusion in the USDA's Grassland Reserve program—"a tiny part of the Farm Bill that does a lot of good stuff"—which aims to protect two million acres of grassland, pasture, and shrubland all over the country from being developed for crops or other uses, including urban development. Designed to retain and restore habitats for animals and plants, the program places a special emphasis on what it calls "working grazing operations," or pastureland like Elizabeth's.

The rest of her seventy-five-acre farm, made up of woodlands and wetlands, is part of the Connecticut Farmland Trust, which holds agricultural easements on about twelve hundred acres of family farms throughout the state, preventing their development as well. In 2007 the organization estimated that in the previous two decades Connecticut had lost twenty-one percent of its farmland at a rate of eight thousand acres per year. Elizabeth was thrilled that her acres would now never be among them. "We didn't want the land to be developed ever," she said, "and the only way you can do that is to put a permanent easement on it. It's what's most important to us."

This echoed something Mark had said earlier, when I

commented that the cheese business seemed to be thriving. "We're about the animals," he said simply. "We're a farm." Now I understood that the cheese was merely the means to a larger end, which was preserving land. The land could be preserved only because Elizabeth used it to pasture the cows, who in turn made it possible to produce the cheese, which provided the money to tend to them and the land—a perfect circle connecting people, food, and farm.

Elizabeth confirmed this when I asked how she had become interested in making cheese instead of just running a dairy farm. She said the cheesemaking was the best way she could think of to keep the farm up and running and even make a little profit. Then she told me about her father, a doctor and also a self-proclaimed "cheesehead." "During World War II, he served in France," she began. "At one point during the fighting, a group of soldiers came running to him and said 'We've found this awful place, you have to come condemn it so we can blow it up.'" Here she paused for effect, then cracked up, her laughter ringing out across the fields. "Well, of course, it was a cheese cave!"

The sky began to spit rain as we wandered back down the road between the pastures. Banks of gray-blue clouds set off the wet, vivid grass. I thought of my own father, who had once failed to return my phone calls for three days because he was in bed after overdosing on the French cheese he had just smuggled home from Europe in his suitcase. "But it was so good!" he had half-moaned (whether out of happiness or nausea I wasn't sure) when he finally managed to dial my number.

On the way back to my car, we stopped at the barn again to visit the new calves in their pens, including a pair of twins and Gin's latest offspring, Vodka. When I reached in to touch their soft brown heads they butted up against my hand and looked at me hopefully, as if I could feed them while they waited for their mothers.

We found Mark outside the cheese shed, loading up the van to be driven to Manhattan before dawn the next morning, to the Saturday greenmarket in Union Square. I thanked him for letting me tag along through the cheesemaking. "Sure," he replied, grinning. "You should get to know what your farmers are doing."

I couldn't resist asking Mark about the cheese preferences of his elder daughter, who wasn't much older than Jules. I imagined him coming home from work with a big hunk of Bloomsday or Hooligan, and his daughter, the child of an honest maker of delicious, hormone-free cow's-milk cheese, relishing every bite, the opposite of my own obstinate eater.

"Oh," he said with a wry smile. "She really likes goat cheese."

I left the farm and drove home with a very full stomach and a light heart.

4

❖

School for Chefs

"Ipswich clams! sooooo good!" David was rhapsodizing one sticky-hot summer afternoon when I arrived in the kitchen. He waved a white plastic container full of the Massachusetts delicacy in the air. "We're going to serve them fried in beer batter with arugula from upstate."

As an eater, I greeted this news with anticipation—surely there would be a clam or two available for kitchen consumption. As the person who was, I suddenly realized, about to spend the evening dunking slimy clams in goopy batter and frying them to order at the garde manger station while also assembling salads, cheese plates, and other appetizers, I was pretty sure I wouldn't make it through the night without a major grease fire. It didn't help that the night before Noah and I had watched an episode of the British spy series *MI-5* in which an operative is murdered by having her head pushed into a deep fryer.

I had not quite managed, at this point, to work up the

degree of passion for cooking that led all of the chefs in the applewood kitchen to create dishes that required first a lot of prep and then even more work after they were ordered. They were excited about the possibilities of food and wanted to experiment all the time; if some delicious new combination required three or four extra steps in the pickup—the cooking that gets done when the dish is "fired," meaning the table that ordered it has finished the previous course—they didn't mind. Why make food that you could assemble with minimum ease and potential for burning yourself when you could do it the hard way? The clams were a minor example of this kind of thing. On other occasions I watched David poach eggs to go on top of a pork-belly appetizer while simultaneously sautéing mushrooms for one dish, making caper butter for another, and roasting fish for a third. Because almost all the dishes were new every night, there was no opportunity to get really good at making something (or at least, for me to get really good at it, since the chefs were already pretty good at making anything they could think up). As soon as you—that is, I—learned to make pan-seared scallops with spinach, milk-poached garlic, and a splash of Concord grape reduction by cooking it fifteen times in one night, it was off the menu.

So it would be, I knew, with the clams. The spattering of oil wouldn't start until about four-thirty, when we would make a batch to test the batter and let everyone try them. In the meantime, I got busy peeling avocados for a salad with pickled watermelon rind (the product of someone's pawing through the walk-in for a project during a slow dinner service), cleaning a big box of arugula, and wincing each time someone new came in, saw the fryer, and gave me a look of pity.

As always, family meal was served to all of us—waitstaff, chefs, dishwashers—at three-thirty. That day it was pork and duck meatloaf, which gave a whole new meaning to the word "leftovers." Unlike so-called family meals at my house, everyone not only ate what was offered but also graciously thanked Liza, who had somehow found time to make the meatloaf, along with a salad, while also prepping for dinner. When family meal was over, we filled the fryer with canola oil and cranked it up to start heating. David mixed up a batch of batter and got the clams out of his lowboy again. Each viscous glob was gray, with a roughly nickel-sized body attached to a gooey substance that dripped and slid between my fingers like cold gelatin. I put on a plastic glove, picked up five clams, and dropped them into the batter. Then I plunged my hand into the mixture to fish them out, a horribly oozy search-and-rescue mission. I finally managed to capture them and dump them into the simmering oil, where they sizzled and spattered and turned into frilly little golden blobs within about a minute. As I scooped them up with a perforated spoon (miraculously, without burning myself) and dropped them onto paper towels to drain, I worried about how I could possibly cook batch after batch of them to the perfect combination of tender and crisp when the orders started coming in. I had quickly learned that there was a restaurant version of Murphy's Law: if there was something particularly complicated on the menu, everyone would order it. This seemed to be doubly true when there was something complicated on the menu and I was in charge of making it.

Then we all tasted the clams and suddenly it didn't matter how hard they were to fry properly or how much money David had spent on them when he could have gotten lesser clams at a lower price. "It's like licking the boardwalk," said one of the servers, a look of sublime pleasure on his face. Just then Laura came into the kitchen in a pre-dinner funk. "I don't want one!" she said in a stressed tone when David offered a clam. "You should taste it," he replied calmly. "It tastes like the Atlantic Ocean." That was enough to break Laura's pique. In the summer the Sheas spend their precious days off on Cape Cod, and David was willing to say these clams were as good as being at the shore with Tatum and Sophie. Laura popped one in her mouth and bit down into its soft, briny center. "Oh. That's good," she sighed as she walked, newly serene, back to the office.

As I had predicted, the minute customers read the menu, they all ordered clams. Everyone, it seemed, wanted to be transported to his or her favorite seaside haunt in a single bite. Over and over the servers came through the swinging door yelling, "Fire two clams! Fire three clams!" as they stuck their tickets on the rail in front of me. The rest of the kitchen staff didn't even try to hide their relief that someone else was the sucker up to her elbow in batter, peering into a vat of boiling oil in the middle of a heat wave.

But then it was no picnic over at the stove, either. Once the dinner rush started, all the burners were left blazing to save the hassle of turning them on and off—a task that was a special kind of hassle at applewood because the stove had no actual burner knobs. Instead, it had burning-hot metal stubs that had once held knobs. To light a burner you had to grab the stub with a towel and twist it to get the gas flowing, then ignite it with a wand lighter.

"Is this a restaurant thing?" I finally asked one night after wrestling with an especially sticky stub.

"No, it's an applewood thing," said Liza, who seemed unfazed by the knoblessness. David and his father had bought the stove second hand for eight hundred dollars, which is apparently a great deal as long as you're willing to accept a few minor flaws. Like no knobs.

It was so hot at the stove that night that a conversation began about the spontaneous combustion of chef's jackets. "Oh, I've been in hotter places," David said. Flipping a duck breast over at the grill, he continued, "In the Navy, the night before firefighting training, they tell you to wear cotton underwear because anything synthetic will melt right to your skin." Suddenly, whining about the waves of oily heat emanating from the clam fryer seemed inadvisable. At least my hand cooled off whenever I dipped it in the batter.

"You were in the Navy?" the latest kitchen extern said incredulously.

David just smiled and drained the duck breast.

On a shelf in Sophie and Tatum's old room beneath the office loft sits a small photograph of a baby-faced, blue-eyed teenager in a sailor suit with a white sailor hat perched on his dark hair and the American flag behind him. This was David in 1987, when, after dropping out of high school, he joined the Navy to save himself. "I'm not one of those guys that went into the kitchen at twelve years old and spent their life there," he told me once. "I joined the Navy when I was seventeen. I had been living on my own, doing my own thing, and getting into trouble. Thankfully I was smart enough to realize I was getting into *real* trouble and I needed to do something else, so I got my parents to sign me away."

He went directly from the West Village to the famous recruiting booth in Times Square to enlist, and from there went on to boot camp. In the Navy he earned his GED and was trained to fuel jets on aircraft carriers. ("Not very practical in the real world. You can get a job at an airport.") Discharged at twenty, he found work fishing for cod in Alaska and then, back in New York, did a stint as a locksmith and worked in several low-end restaurants making pasta and pizza.

"I just found that I had a knack for it in the most uneducated, basic way," he remembered of his first forays into cooking. "I got to the point where I didn't want to continue at that level. I tried to break into the next tier of restaurant but nobody wanted anything to do with me. I didn't have anything serious on my resume, I didn't know the terminology, I had no classical training at all." It was the mid-1990s, before the Food Network or celebrity chefs, and cooking school was nowhere near as trendy as it has since become, but David realized that if he wanted to move up he needed to study. When he was accepted to the Culinary Institute of America, his grandmother agreed to pay his tuition for the first semester, after which, if he stayed, he would be on his own. He paid for the remaining semesters until graduation with student loans.

Taking classes on everything from making consommé to baking bread, he saw that they were hugely challenging for many of the other students. For David, though, the skills came naturally. "I was good at it for whatever reason. Not by any effort of my own, more genetics or just something that works for me. So I was able to cruise through school. I loved it. I learned a lot."

After he and Laura finished school they moved to Chicago, where he had a series of jobs cooking at fine-dining restaurants, then to New York, where he had one memorably awful job making burgers before they decided to strike out on their own. All along David knew he wanted to have his own restaurant, and that when he did, the kind of natural ease he'd felt in cooking school was what he'd look for when hiring kitchen staff.

Indeed, cooking school wasn't required for success at applewood, as Liza had proved. When I asked why she hadn't gone, she said, "They don't teach you how to make food and create food. They don't teach you anything you couldn't learn on your own with a few reference books and working under a few good chefs. It would be much more useful if they taught you how to *think* about food." She had worked in a number of high-end Manhattan restaurants, and had landed at applewood largely because she could experiment and imagine to her heart's content. "This is the only place where they let you create your own food from day one," she told me. "'Here's the meat station: write your menu.'"

Also not an alumnus of cooking school was Greg, who was working part time when I started at applewood and had become David's number two by the time I left. His first job in New York had been at a restaurant owned by the brother of a school friend. "They said, 'Do you want to be a busboy or learn to cook?' I chose learn to cook. I just stood on the line for the first three weeks. I didn't even know how to peel a potato."

Sarah of candied orange peel fame, over at the grill, had gone to cooking school and done her externship at applewood, but along with her more traditional credentials, she brought something novel to David's kitchen. Originally trained in theater, she had a kind of presence that none of the others did, her long brown hair bound up underneath a bright scarf, her conversation interspersed with hearty exclamations of "Delicious!" While the rest of us limited ourselves to mumbling along off-key with the eighties hits blaring from the kitchen radio during afternoon prep work, Sarah was not afraid to break into food-related song, occasionally belting out a line or two as she went about chopping onions or some other task. More than once I heard her sing about what she was plating—"This meat is very well done," to the tune of the last song we'd heard on the radio before dinner service began, or a high, melodic "Onions!" as she spooned cipollini ragout into a bowl. During a particularly intricate maneuver that involved pouring pickling liquid from a wide-mouthed container into a small-mouthed one, she produced a little aria with the lyric "This is going to end badly!" And she was absolutely right.

This small group of people, all of whom were referred to as "Chef" (subverting the traditional kitchen structure in which only David would have had that title, and leading to hilarious conversations that began, "Chef?" "Yes, Chef?"), brought a range of personal variation to the food they prepared, and David liked it that way even as he held them to a very high standard. Of course they all absorbed a certain ethos and aesthetic just by watching him cook, but there were days when he had no hand at all in writing the menu. Every dish was cleared with him, but with total confidence in his chefs and in the quality of their ingredients, he was happy to let them experiment the same way he experimented. Every person who came through the kitchen in my time at applewood told me that this attitude made working there unlike working anywhere else.

Andrew, August's predecessor at the pastry station, put it best. He was about to leave applewood, only because he had been offered his dream job, tending to an organic rooftop garden at a private school and cooking for the students. While helping to interview candidates to replace him, he remarked that at other restaurants, even—or perhaps especially—famous ones, "you don't get to have any ideas. That's why we're getting résumés from people who are at great places." Just that day he had talked to an applicant who worked at one of Manhattan's most exclusive restaurants and was eager to escape to a job where everything wasn't the same all the time. All these people already had their training; they were longing for a chance to really deploy it. Restaurant life was taxing enough—the long hours, the stress, the heat—without having to execute someone else's idea of short ribs night after night after night. David encouraged his kitchen colleagues to look at the food in front of them and invent, and he inspired them by example as much as by anything he said.

I benefited from this as well. One afternoon David gave me a crate of parsnips, then showed me how to chop them so they came out in what he called "funny little pieces," angular, asymmetrical bits. First he peeled the parsnip, then he started cutting it at an angle, turning it toward him about a quarter-rotation after each chop, going around and around so that it looked like the point of a pencil as it shed piece after piece. "It's called an oblique cut," David said. "That's what the asshole French cooking teacher would tell you." Then he watched me chop for a minute or two, offering advice. "A little bigger." Chop. "A little harsher angle." Chop. "Perfection!" And even though I knew it wasn't perfect at all, and that I was very slow in creating even imperfect pieces, it was passable.

A more dictatorial chef might have made me consign all the rather haphazard parsnip fragments to quarts to be used for parsnip purée or even family meal, but not David. I realized as he left me to my chopping that I had begun to internalize the ethos of his kitchen on my own terms. I didn't have to do everything exactly the way David would have done it; I did have to do my best. My parsnip pieces were many different sizes and lacked the elegance they would have had if he'd been the chopper, but he was willing to accept them. In cooking school I would have been made to perform this task over and over again until I could produce pieces of uniform size and angles. (The externs and recent graduates all had stories of being in tears over, for example, endlessly practicing tournée-cut potatoes, the peeled ones shaped like little footballs, at home late at night, in order to pass a class.) At applewood, David allowed us time and space to improve.

Often when I watched David visiting the various stations and answering younger chefs' and externs' questions, encouraging them to try things and see what happened, I saw the kitchen as a kind of teaching hospital for chefs, myself included. Once when I asked about how he came up with new dishes, David shrugged and said, "You can't do it right, you can't do it wrong." He never lost his temper at me even when I made idiotic mistakes like forgetting to take those theoretically oblique-cut parsnips out of the oven during prep so that they emerged as, rather than tender little bits, semi-charred fragments that David dubbed "parsnip chips." (We salvaged them with shocking amounts of heavy cream, and they were a big hit at dinner that night.)

David himself had been screamed at mercilessly by the chef at one fancy restaurant where he worked. "They're all so macho," he sighed, remembering. "I had been a seventeen-year-old kid in boot camp, intimidated, scared. After that, being bossed around in some restaurant seems ridiculous. I was never into that. After being in the Navy it just seemed absurd to be yelled at in a kitchen."

None of which is to say that applewood's kitchen was entirely free of conflicts. Liza departed about five months into my stay after a kind of subterranean turf war that rose to the surface after she returned from a vacation. No one wanted to discuss it, but I thought that during her absence David might have begun to feel he had ceded too much power to her, or she might have realized she was ready to run her own kitchen (as she went on to do), or, most likely, some combination of the two. Still, I was taken completely by surprise when David told me she was gone, having caught no whiff of trouble in my recent shifts. I did hear that David lost his temper every now and then, but that he always apologized. He didn't relish getting angry at all. "He made me so mad I actually yelled at him," he confided in me once about an unsatisfactory extern. "He ruined six pounds of butter, and then he lied about it. I mean okay, ruin six pounds of butter, it's not the end of the world. But don't do it and say you ruined three!"

But such moments were rare, and the kitchen itself was never tense, even during the craziest dinner rush, the kind I experienced full-on as I flailed over the clam fryer that hot summer night. That was when I noticed for the first time the motto printed on a magnet stuck to the stainless steel shelving to my left. In my frenzy of clam goo and burned batter bits floating in oil, it stood out like a beacon:

Peace. It does not mean to be in a place
where there is no noise, trouble, or hard work.
It means to be in the midst of those things
and still be calm in your heart.

My family was about to leave for Southern California, to spend a month in Noah's hometown, and that motto seemed like a good thought to take along. Maybe, in the serenity of a small beach town, we would all find our centers: Noah and I would stop worrying about what Jules was eating, and Jules would stop refusing to even taste what was on his plate. Noah, who grew up in the surf and believes in the supreme powers of sun, sand, and Mexican food, was betting he could get Jules to eat guacamole and fish tacos at the very least. We flew west with hope in our hearts and peace on our minds.

During that month, the first anniversary of my father's death came around. Noah took me to the beach where he had surfed as a kid, and I threw a bunch of roses into the tide and watched them ride out to sea on the waves. Jules learned to swim underwater, went to the zoo, made friends with his cousins' dogs—and, at a Fourth of July picnic, refused to eat hot dogs, a buttered roll (too close to toast), and even ice cream. (I took this last rejection personally.)

As it turned out, he did expand his palate by a single item that summer: baseball stadium roasted peanuts. I decided to be glad they were at least seasonal in some sense of the word, and I counted the days until I would be back in the kitchen.

❖ Oblique-Cut Caramelized Parsnips
(including emergency Parsnip Chips variation)

5–6 parsnips
½ pound butter, chopped into pieces
salt and pepper

1. Preheat oven to 350 degrees.
2. Peel parsnips and chop obliquely (see page 73).
3. Spread parsnip pieces in a metal roasting pan and scatter butter throughout, then add salt and pepper to taste.
4. Roast for about 30 minutes, stirring occasionally, until golden brown and still tender.

Variation:

If you accidentally roast the parsnips until they are more crispy than tender, remove them immediately to a pot on the stove. Add 1 cup cream to the disaster and cook the whole thing down until the parsnips are tender again, then serve. They'll never know.

Serves 4 as a side.

5

❖

Meet the Farmer

IN AUGUST we returned to the East Coast and the humidity. Jules, who had survived the summer quite happily on his peanut-based diet and even grown an inch, refused to eat chocolate cake at his grandmother's birthday party, though he had a great time yelling "Cake!" whenever someone else took a bite. What he did eat one day when Noah brought him by the restaurant was some crunchy puffed rice with cayenne pepper that Liza had made as a soup garnish. After they left I tasted some and realized it was insanely spicy. This was the start of what we came to refer to as Jules's cocktail party phase, during which he seemed to subsist almost entirely on intensely flavored foods that would ordinarily be found on side tables at adult gatherings—dry roasted nuts, hummus with carrots, red pepper strips, pita chips, unbelievably sour cornichon pickles, and, perhaps oddest of all, pickled cocktail onions. He developed a fondness for this last item at around eighteen months, shortly after he discovered that his father drank martinis. He became Noah's assistant barkeep, delivering drinks and helping shake what he christened a Papatini. Sometimes when I slept in and Noah got up with Jules, I would come into the dining room to find Jules sitting on the floor with an array of vodka, gin, and bourbon bottles, pretending to pour drinks while Noah read the paper in peace at the dining room table, pausing every so often to accept a pretend cocktail.

I went back to applewood as soon as we returned from California. It was miserably hot, and everyone in the kitchen invented reasons to stand in the walk-in for a few minutes, where the temperature was perfect and the produce was amazing. One farm, Lucky Dog Organics in Hamden, New York, was growing vegetables I had never seen before. One week, in preparation for a Meet the Farmer dinner with Lucky Dog's owners, Richard and Holley Giles, we got bronze oak lettuce, purple beans, Red Bor kale, rainbow chard, tomatillos, mixed squash, and beets. The lettuce looked a bit like sea coral—green with rusty edges and little tendrils. It was as frilly as old lace and tore just as easily. The tomatillos looked like miniature Japanese lanterns, their green-and-yellow paper skins rustling as I picked them up. Shucking them revealed pale, almost fluorescent green orbs that were sticky to the touch. I cut one into wedges to try, and it tasted like a slightly harder, lemon-infused tomato, as bright and fresh as the color of its skin.

At the Meet the Farmer dinner, which I attended as a writer rather than a chef, I sat with Richard and Holley. When I mentioned my book project, Richard gave me a sly smile and said, in his mellow drawl (he was originally from Mississippi), "We'll find you a pair of boots if you come up to the farm."

It was an offer I couldn't refuse.

A few weeks later I drove to Lucky Dog on a stormy afternoon that happened to be September 11. On the three-hour trip from the city through the pouring rain, I had plenty of time to listen to somber radio essays and debates about all the promises made after the World Trade Center fell, when we all vowed we were going to stop being so busy, we were going to spend more time with our friends and families, we were going to get back to what really mattered.

Unsurprisingly, a lot of those wistful thoughts about connecting with one another led to food. As the chef and author Mark Bittman wrote in his *New York Times* column days after the towers collapsed, "With all the uncertainty outside, the idea of spending an evening inside, at home among friends, has never seemed more appealing." This was his lead-up to a dinner party menu that involved only minimal time away from the guests because, as he put it, "I wanted time to talk, and I knew they would as well."

Times of crisis have often been times for reconsidering food. In *How to Cook a Wolf,* written in the midst of World War II, M. F. K. Fisher reminded her readers of something she worried they might have forgotten as a result of all the rationing: "Wise men forever have known that a nation lives on what its body assimilates, as well as on what its mind acquires as knowledge. Now, when the hideous necessity of the war machine takes steel and cotton and humanity, our own private personal secret mechanism must be stronger, for selfish comfort as well as for the good of the ideals we believe we believe in." Food is as good a defense as any against the outside world. The way we prepare it and offer it to others says as much about who we are as the way we dress or talk.

These thoughts carried me up to Hamden, in the Delaware River valley, where I parked in front of the Lucky Dog Farm Store, located in one of the trim little houses lining Main Street. I wondered where the farm could possibly be; no open land was visible nearby. I went into the store and there was Holley behind the counter, a pretty, petite Texan with long brown hair and an open face who looked far younger than her forty-three years.

"You found us!" she said. "Come on, I'll take you to Richard."

We went out the back door, through a gate in a chain-link fence, down some stone steps, and there it was: forty-four acres spread out in a green vista below me with the West Branch of the Delaware running along behind it and the Catskill Mountains rising above. A line of orange and red tractors and harvesters sat near an old red barn with two silos and several plastic-covered hoop houses. I felt, once again, as if I had stumbled down the rabbit hole, this time by way of an ordinary storefront.

"Hey there," said Richard, wiping his muddy hands on his pants as he walked toward me. He was tall and lanky, with shoulder-length, slightly graying dark-blond hair and a chiseled face. "We're doing rainy day work. Come on."

He and the farm crew were laying some new concrete floor in the barn (which was used for washing and packing produce rather than housing animals), doing equipment maintenance, and cutting weeds. Holley headed back to the store, and I sat on a soggy pile of uprooted plants watching Richard pull up and hack away at another stand. "We're slogging through the mud," he said, grinning. "We all tend to have kind of an artificial view of farms because we like the 'big farm' look—not many weeds, just beautiful crops in the field. That's become our ideal, instead of lots of personality, lots of people, lots of energy, lots of unpleasant work." As if on cue, Micah, one of the farmhands, came over to talk about the next day's potato harvest, which was going to be incredibly muddy thanks to all the rain. "We're all kind of dreading it," Richard said, but there was a lightness to his voice that implied otherwise.

Looking around, I could see why. Even pummeled by rain, the fields were gorgeous and lush. I was swept up in the romance of the whole enterprise—living off the land, raising children with a true sense of what food is—though I knew my vision of what that meant was probably false. (Later in my visit, Holley told me she liked raising her kids, Sybilla and Asa, who were then six and three years old, on the farm, but wished they had "a little more appreciation for the vegetables.") Richard, who must have seen the look in my eye, threw me a bone. "We have eagles," he said, gesturing upwards. "The least sentimental person on the crew will look up while we're picking crops and say 'It looks *good* out here.'" He continued, "I love being out. I love farming. We were going to keep working in New York and work this into a place where we could live. Then Holley quit her job within a few weeks. Within six months I quit mine and we wound up here."

In their previous life in Brooklyn, Richard had taught writing and Holley had worked in publishing. In 1999, when they first saw the former dairy farm that would become Lucky Dog, the land was being rented by a neighboring farmer who was using it to grow corn; its owners had sold their cows eight years earlier. Richard could tell by the cornstalk stubble remaining from a recent harvest that it was a good piece of ground, and the next day he made an offer for the house, barn, and cropland.

Unlike Holley, who wanted to get out of the city to raise a family and figured farming was a way to make a living, Richard comes from a farming family, albeit one of a different kind from the one he's in now. His father, an agronomist at Mississippi State University, oversaw a USDA experimental research program that focused on cotton, rice, and soybean production. "A lot of the research was about chemicals," Richard recalled. "The air smelled of chemistry. From the window of the school bus, at some time each year, we would see thousands of fish floating belly-up in Deer Creek, the bayou that runs through Washington County. People would be down on the banks with poles and nets pulling out the poisoned fish."

Richard got a degree in animal science at Mississippi State and started managing operations on large beef cattle farms in the area. Slowly he discovered that his true calling lay elsewhere. At one of the large farms he had the opportunity to plant a soybean crop, and eventually he bought a small farm in Monroe County, Mississippi, where he spent a year growing vegetables and selling them locally. He loved it, but he and his first wife had a young family and it was difficult, uncertain work, so he went back to a large farm, "where I could get a paycheck." He stayed in that job until his marriage unraveled, at which point, looking for a change, he went to graduate school and on to teaching.

At the time, he said now, "I didn't intend to teach forever, but I didn't intend to go back to the farm." He landed in Brooklyn, where he built a life but still somehow found himself "waiting for just the right farm to come along." He spent weekends driving around the Catskills looking for property. Soon he met Holley, who joined the farm search enthusiastically, and they ended up at Lucky Dog, which Holley named in honor of their three rescue dogs.

They knew from the start that they wanted to farm organically. For fertilizing and pest control, Lucky Dog uses only materials approved by OMRI, the Organic Materials Review Institute (an independent organization that tests products intended to be used in certified organic farming).

These include a pesticide called Spinosad, made from a natural bacterium, which attacks potato beetles without harming
beneficial insects like ladybugs; hydrogen peroxide on things
like seed potatoes, wash surfaces, and the leaves of tomato
plants; and other basic elements like ground limestone to improve soil quality.

"One of the happiest things about finding and operating
this farm," Richard told me, "is that it's a continuation of
that beginning of a little vegetable farm that I started in Mississippi. I love growing food that we can all eat, and I love
the fact that I can grow it without killing fish or going back
to what I think is the wrong road of commodity agriculture.
So it's also quite terrifying that this is almost not working,
that the returns are so slim and the risks so high that it isn't
sound business."

Those risks, as Richard detailed them without any self-
pity during my stay at Lucky Dog, made me embarrassed
that I had ever complained about the price of produce at my
local farmers' market. In order to function, most farmers, especially small ones, borrow money every year for operations
and hope they'll be able to at least break even and pay it back
by selling their crops. In Lucky Dog's case, the majority of
sales come through farmers' markets and wholesale orders
from places like applewood, and another ten percent come
through the Community Supported Agriculture (CSA) program, in which local people pay ahead for shares of what the
farm grows, which they receive weekly during the harvest
season.

Sometimes, though, there's nothing to sell. In the summer of 2006, Lucky Dog was entirely flooded out in a torrential rainstorm, and Richard and Holley lost their whole season of produce. They found, however, that they were not alone. "We got tremendous support," Richard remembered, shaking his head in disbelief. "Customer after customer sent us checks or handed us checks. People bought two or three years ahead at the CSA." In Brooklyn, applewood threw a benefit cocktail party with a silent auction of items donated by people from the neighborhood, some close friends of Richard's or Holley's, and many who didn't know them but felt connected to them through the food they ate at the restaurant. But even with the outpouring of support, Richard told me, "We're a tiny farm and we lost so much it was very hard to recover." He paused. "We lost so much."

Then he took me over to the side of one of the hoop houses and showed me the floodwater mark about three feet above the ground. I looked at the fields, now bursting with vegetables in the early autumn sun, and imagined them covered by water, not even the tops of the chard showing. "We paid our crew," he said, "but we couldn't pay back our operating loan and had to refinance. We're going to feel it for years. We have a forty-thousand-dollar loan payment due in January and we only have about eighteen thousand, so I'm getting anxious about that."

Besides the precarious finances of small organic farms, Richard also faced the larger issue of a produce market that, as he put it in an email conversation we had later, "takes for granted the abundance of blemish-free produce . . . and has lost the habits of patience and acceptance. Beautiful food in huge quantities at very low prices is a daunting competitor for beautiful organically grown food seasonally available at prices that would reflect a real return to the people who grow it. The real costs of growing organic food are higher than the prices it brings."

This is something people don't like to hear, but Richard welcomes the chance to discuss it with anyone, whatever their reasons for buying his produce. "When we were selling to the greenmarket in New York [Union Square], we took kale," he recalled with a chuckle that afternoon on the weed pile. "One weekend we sold out in an hour and we said, 'What's going on with kale?' It turned out the *New York Times* had just run an article about how great kale is."

Becoming serious again, he added, "I've heard people down in New York City talking about eating local. The primary thing is, what does it mean to support local farms? It's not just buying from them. Supporting local farms now means supporting the building of an infrastructure. My hope is that people will come to my stand and talk, to say that food is expensive. Then we could talk about what food and where."

Richard believes most people are still unaware of the hidden price of conventional agriculture, which is never passed on directly at the market in the same way as the costs of growing on a small, organic farm. "The costs of growing organically are much more visible, more basic, more demonstrable," he told me. "With conventionally grown food, the cost is less easy to see. There's the public funding of the great western water impoundment projects to irrigate the desert, and there's the interstate highway system that supports trucking across an impossible distance. We've all agreed to pay these costs by levy." (In this I heard the distinct echo of farmer Joel Salatin, who told Michael Pollan something very similar. In *The Omnivore's Dilemma* Pollan quoted Salatin as saying, "Whenever I hear people say clean food is expensive, I tell them it's actually the cheapest food you can buy." Then he added, "With our food all of the costs are figured into the price. Society is not bearing the cost of water pollution, of antibiotic resistance, of food-borne illnesses, of crop subsidies, of subsidized oil and water—all of the hidden costs to the environment and the taxpayer that make cheap food seem cheap.")

As the sun moved across the sky above the hills and the guys in the barn finished pouring the concrete for the new floor, Richard grew passionate. "These little farms around here have to be farms again. You have a community again then. You share equipment and labor. You build an economy that is based on the dirt. And you have a hopeful alliance when someone in a town meeting says, out of fear and idiocy and boredom, that farming is dead." Hamden, he told me, was suffering from a kind of generalized hopelessness as a result of the poor economic conditions. "So I'm willing to deal every weekend with customers who want my organic food because it's good for their health, but I'm anxious that the real things get addressed. I keep trying to turn every conversation not just to local food but to the system we all support. When someone offers to support our farm by buying our goods, I'm happy but I try to steer the conversation to price, the value of organic food, and possibly even to the idea that they might consider some capital support of the farm."

I couldn't help mentioning the guilt I felt at the supermarket over exactly these kinds of issues, the way I still sometimes debated about whether I should buy anything imported at all, or anything that I might be able to get a few days later at the farmers' market, even if it meant an extra stop on a busy weekend. It was sometimes hard, in those moments, to keep in mind what was at stake. But even as I expressed those concerns to Richard, I realized that my indecision was starting to fade. Much in the same way that Jules's birth had made the health issues real to me, the people and places I was visiting, applewood included, were making an intricate web of eating, environment, and community newly clear to me.

Still, I couldn't see how it was possible to support every part of this web all the time, which I confessed to Richard. "I think there's a compromise and we all make it," he said in response. "New Yorkers live in one of the most efficient cities in the world. We can't compare. We heat the house all winter. Our driving efficiencies are poor. And I love to have oranges in the morning from Florida. I think trying to be aware and do the right thing . . ."—here he stopped cutting weeds to think for a second. "I don't think just these per-sonal purchasing choices are all you're talking about. We're going to have to start advocating for farmers. That means asking our land grant universities to help us figure out how to grow good clean food. It means calling out the money to support clean agriculture in the New York City watershed. It means providing basic funding to the farms themselves—capitalizing land and major equipment. It means preserva-tion of farmland with development easements and outright purchases."

I thought of Cato Corner when he said this, of Elizabeth MacAlister's great pleasure in the knowledge that her land would be kept as it was in perpetuity. Part of helping farm-ers like her and Richard was, as he said, buying their prod-ucts, which kept their farms operational. But it was also im-portant to know why the buying mattered on a larger level, what that extra fifty cents or a dollar was going toward—saving a piece of land or perhaps even a whole way of life in a place like Hamden. "We've substituted fossil fuels and fake fertilizers and poisons for what any real farmer knows must be honored as a complex living system," Richard continued. "Everything is disposable, including the farmer and his labor and even the land. Organic farming systems are or certainly should be aiming toward a system of saving and recycling—fertility from natural sources, plowing down of unused ma-terials to build the life of the soil, saving rather than spending or discarding, and honoring the human labor in the crop. We can grow the food we need to eat around the world, but the profit centers are going to be small and local, not large and conglomerate."

Just then Sybilla appeared, fresh off the school bus, blond and pixie-like, her face a miniature version of her mother's. "Hi, Chickadee. How was school?" Richard asked, giving her a hug before she climbed up the pile of gravel that would be added to the new barn floor. Then she invited me to the house to look at the newly hatched Monarch butterfly she had living in a wooden salad bowl with three more cocoons. Richard looked as if he had some work to do that didn't involve talking to an inquisitive visitor, so Sybilla and I went up the stone steps toward the house, accompanied by three dogs named Oz, Lucy, and Gizmo.

I spent the rest of the afternoon with Sybilla, having a tea party and helping her try to feed raisins to her butterfly. I had asked Richard whether or not growing up on an organic farm made a difference when it came to his kids' eating habits, and his story was, if not quite as dire as mine, very similar to Laura's. "They both started out eating everything, and we thought it would continue," he said. "But school is a quick educator in how to refuse your vegetables. Our kids know they're farm kids and we let them know about the food. But they probably aren't a bit different from other kids in their preferences. We try to bribe them to eat vegetables. They may refuse to eat their Lucky Dog broccoli, but there's organic rice beside it on the plate. Except when they go to Wendy's with their grandmother or eat school lunch, they always have a wide variety of choices of local and organic food."

Just knowing that even the children of organic farmers sometimes ate fast food was a huge relief. After our tea party, when Sybilla and I were put to work shelling fresh-picked tongue-of-fire beans for dinner, removing them from their ivory-and-maroon-streaked pods—beans that, I now suspected, neither she nor Asa would touch—I hoped she might offer up her perspective on farm life.

"Do you like living on a farm?" I began, not quite sure how to interview a six-year-old.

"Yes." This was the first of what turned out to be a series of responses as efficient as telegrams and delivered with the same declarative force.

"Why?"

"Because we have lots of yummy vegetables."

"You like that?"

"Yes."

"Why?"

"Because we can pick them ourselves and we don't have to buy them at the store." At last she was warming up!

"Why is that good?"

"Because we don't have to buy the not-organic ones."

I wondered how much she really knew about organic produce, and if she had talked about it with school friends— was this a topic kids discussed at recess these days?

"Do you have friends who live on farms?"

"Yes."

And then, before I could begin to craft a follow-up question wily enough to get this master of brevity to say a bit more, she spoke again, with all the studied precision of a politician trying to get a point across without naming any names.

"Well, she's not really a friend. She's mean sometimes."

Interview over.

Dinner that night was all from the farm. The tongue-of-fire beans, which had been streaked like their pods when raw but were beige after cooking and had a mellow, nutty taste, were accompanied by fried white and purple potatoes, mixed salad, corn off the cob sautéed with garlic, and bread Holley had made. It was delicious; each vegetable on my plate tasted like a different facet of the same lazy summer afternoon (though I would learn the next day that there is no such thing as a lazy summer afternoon on a farm).

Asa and Sybilla, I was gratified to see, stayed in their chairs only marginally longer than Jules would have (Holley diagnosed the problem as "showing off for the company"), and they hardly ate a thing. Instead, they spent a lot of time talking about *The Wizard of Oz,* which they referred to as "The Dorothy Movie." Later in the evening we all piled onto a futon upstairs to watch the last half hour of the film, and when it was over Sybilla tried to persuade me to sleep in her bed with her since the pouring rain had scotched my plans to camp by the river.

Instead, I drove half a mile down the road to a motel. As I set my alarm for five-fifteen the next morning, anticipating exhaustion, my only solace was that Noah would probably be up about half an hour later, fielding demands for Cheerios and bananas—and for puffed cayenne rice, which he would not be able to produce.

❖ Puffed Cayenne Rice

6 cups canola oil
2 cups wild rice
salt
cayenne pepper

1. Heat canola oil over medium heat in a deep, heavy pot until a piece of rice dropped in sizzles.

2. Add rice to canola oil and deep-fry for approximately 5 minutes.

3. Remove rice using a long-handled perforated spoon and place it on paper towels to drain and cool.

4. Toss rice in a bowl or pan with salt and cayenne pepper to taste.

Serves many, including one eccentric toddler, as a snack or a soup garnish.

❖ Corn Off the Cob with Garlic

6 ears fresh corn
2–3 cloves garlic
2 tablespoons butter
salt and pepper

1. Shuck corn and slice kernels off cobs into a bowl, starting at the top of each ear and cutting in a downward motion.

2. Mince garlic.

3. Melt butter over medium-low heat in a heavy frying pan large enough to hold all the corn kernels without losing any when you stir them.

4. Add garlic to butter, and after a few seconds, add the corn kernels.

5. Sauté for about 5 minutes, or until the corn looks a little toasted on the edges if you prefer it that way. Season with salt and pepper to taste and serve.

Serves 5 as a side.

6

❖

Lucky Me, Lucky You

HERE'S A THEORY you may not have heard before: working on an organic produce farm is like being in an episode of *I Love Lucy*. More specifically, arriving for work on an organic produce farm in the inky dark of five-thirty in the morning, without any coffee, and being stationed at the bean-sorting machine is exactly like being in the famous episode in which Lucy and Ethel go to work at the chocolate factory and can't keep up with the conveyor belt of chocolates. (Without any coffee. I should probably confess right now that Jules's third word, after "no" and "this," was "coffee.") But I'll get back to that.

When the alarm woke me, I put on as many clothes as I could layer—it was about thirty degrees outside, and pitch black, but the rain had stopped at last—and drove over to the farm. This was after I attempted to open the door to the motel's main office, where the proprietor had assured me there would be coffee set up because "people get up real early around here," only to discover it was locked tight. Early can be a relative term.

When I got to Lucky Dog, the only light I saw was coming from the farthest corner of the barn. Entering the old building, I made my way past various machines used for washing and sorting vegetables, to a small room that served as a makeshift office (dirt-covered fax machine, pens, invoices). There was Richard, wearing a big wool sweater and holding a steaming mug of coffee. "Good morning!" he greeted me cheerfully. "Hi," I said weakly, scanning the room for a coffeemaker that wasn't there. Richard must have brought his from the house, which seemed acres away in the damp, dark morning. I was going to have to suffer my caffeine deprivation in silence.

The farm crew, all of whom were under the age of twenty-five and most of whom came from one local family—yet another way in which Richard was helping to strengthen the community—started straggling in. There was Micah, with curly blond hair and tattoos on his arms, who had discussed the potato harvest with Richard the day before; his fiancée, Alese, wearing pants with stars on the back pockets and newly pregnant with their second child; Alese's brother Kalan, whose wife, Kathleen, worked in the farm store with their six-week-old daughter in tow; Alese and Kalan's sisters Daniele and Ashley; and their aunt Val, who seemed to be about my age and was just working for a day to make some extra money. Richard was happy to have her because we had to pick, wash, and pack the farm's largest order ever—it was the heart of the harvest season and, he said, there was "almost unlimited demand" for his vegetables—by about four o'clock, when the driver from the produce distributor would show up.

By five-forty-five everyone was there. Richard turned on some lights and posted me and three others along the sides of the bean-sorting machine to pick over four crates of the same tongue-of-fire beans I'd eaten at dinner the night before. The machine was like nothing I'd ever seen, made of green-painted metal with a big cylindrical spinning brush at one end of a long bed of corrugated metal. Switched on, the apparatus shook and rattled continuously while someone stood behind the huge brush and emptied crates of beans into a tray beneath it. The brush's bristles picked up the beans, dumping them at a steady rate onto the corrugated bed, where the vibration arranged them into lines in the grooves between the ridges, making it easier to spot and remove rotten, ugly, and broken pods. Propelled by the constant shaking, the sorted beans moved along the metal bed and fell from its end into waiting plastic crates.

For this process to work, though, the people watching the flow of beans needed sharp eyes and incredibly fast hands. I have pretty good hand-eye coordination, honed by, among other things, an abiding love of Ping-Pong, but this was a challenge I found daunting. We stood by the machine, two to a side, watching the beans shimmy and shake their way along the metal bed. To my uncaffeinated eyes, the magenta-streaked pods went by at a rate that was almost impossible to keep up with, even with four of us grabbing at them every few seconds. To look away for even a moment broke my concentration. Sometimes two of us would reach for the same pod, fumble it, and end up letting it move on to fall into the crates. As I focused on snatching beans, the world around me dropped away. After about fifteen minutes I was comfortable enough to start grabbing with both hands—right, left, right, left—throwing the bad pods to the floor without looking down, and doubling my efficiency. A panicky adrenaline rush kept me going, and with it came an eerie sense of déjà vu. I had never worked on a produce farm before, or even visited one, and yet this whole setup seemed familiar.

This was my *I Love Lucy* moment. The grabbing, the comedic desperation—I could almost hear a laugh track in the background. This train of thought led me, naturally, to wishing the beans were chocolates—if I was going to be humbled by a conveyor belt, it should at least have candy on it. And that distraction, in turn, led me to let a few flawed beans go by. Still, the surreal humor of the comparison eased my early-morning weariness. By the time we finished sorting the tongues of fire, light from the rising sun had begun to show in the barn windows.

It was almost seven A.M. when we all put on insulated boots into which we tucked billowing plastic pants—mine were bright yellow—to ward off water and mud and grabbed knives to take to the fields. These knives were about seven inches long and an inch and a half wide, and while they weren't razor sharp, they were definitely capable of doing some serious damage. Nevertheless, most of us dangled them casually from our wrists by the loops of string that ran through holes in their handles, as though they were no more sinister than a pocketbook or a yo-yo (the others stuck them casually in their back pockets, blade down, which terrified me). I wondered, as I had so often in the applewood kitchen, if anyone was worried about handing me a tool I was obviously unequipped to use. But, just as at the restaurant, this thought was swept away by the plain fact that there was a lot of work to be done and no one had time to worry about me. I had two arms and two legs and I could hold a knife, therefore I was worth taking a gamble on.

Sloshing around in our pants and boots, we climbed into two white trucks and drove a little way down the road to some land Richard and Holley were renting in order to grow more crops. It was windy and freezing when we got out, and I noticed enviously that Ashley was wearing a hat. The green fields were faintly iridescent in the day's first light as we hauled plastic crates between the neat rows, spread out one or two people to a row, and started cutting baby spinach leaves. Baby spinach grows very close to the ground, an inch or two high at most, so I had to either bend down over and over as I cut leaves and tossed them into my crate, or else sit in the mud, which was so cold that I could feel its chill through my plastic pants even though they kept me dry. I chose the former. Bend, slice, up. Bend, slice, up. I'd never noticed before how small baby spinach leaves were, or how many it might take to fill a crate. Hundreds? Thousands? Bend, slice, up. Bend, slice, up. Usually nothing bothered my back, not even carrying Jules up and down the four flights of stairs to our apartment many times in a single day, but now it was killing me. I felt like an urban greenhorn. It wasn't even fully daylight yet and already I was aching.

After the spinach we moved on to lettuce. There should be an entire book — and not a seed catalog — about the *names* of lettuce. Over the course of the next hour, we picked Berenice lettuce, Cocarde lettuce, Magenta lettuce (which was a sultry burgundy color and stood out in a dramatic dark swath in the otherwise verdant field), Vulcan lettuce, Galactic lettuce, green and red Salad Bowl lettuces, Nancy lettuce, Red Cross lettuce, and Pirat lettuce. Each head was crisp and beautiful. Each head was also drenched in unbelievably cold water from the overnight storm. I began with Vulcan, great green-and-red heads that bloomed like roses at the center. They grew taller than the spinach, so I was able to squat rather than sit or bend over in the mud. I grabbed each head at the stem, cut it off at the base, removed a few bad outer leaves, and put it in the crate I dragged along as I shuffled sideways to the next lettuce, still squatting.

It wasn't possible to wear gloves while cutting; within minutes my hands were wet and red and so cold they hurt. My fingers swelled and stiffened, and after every few heads I had to stand up (which made me notice how much the work was straining my knees) and warm my hands in the pockets of the jeans I was wearing under my plastic pants until they were usable again. (I didn't see anyone else doing this.) On and on we worked. It took twenty-four lettuces to fill a crate, and that day we filled forty-four crates — one thousand fifty-six lettuces, picked by eight people, in nascent daylight, in mud so deep in places that each of us got stuck in it at least once and had to step out of a mired boot and balance precariously on one foot while tugging at the boot until it came free with a loud sucking sound.

It also took twenty-four bunches of kale, which was our next stop, to fill a crate, and we had twenty crates' worth of those to pick. There were three kinds—Green, Red Russian, and Lacinato, a darker green variety with crinkly leaves. Each plant was about as tall as the lettuce, but looked like a cabbage that had failed to form a head and instead had spread its leaves into a span as wide as two feet. Picking kale was different from picking lettuce because instead of chopping off the whole head you sliced off single leaves, gathering them in your free hand while you kept cutting with the other one. When you had enough for a full bunch—about fifteen leaves, depending on their size—you threw your knife into the crate you were, once again, dragging along, pulled from your pocket a plastic tag provided by Angello's, the farm's produce distributor, and used its rubber loop to band the bunch together.

Each farm Angello's works with gets personalized tags with its name and location on the front and a motto and the farmers' names on the back. The back of Lucky Dog's tags read: "Lucky you, lucky me. Fresh produce from the Catskills. Richard and Holley Giles." After twisting its rubber loop around a bunch of kale—and then, as I'd been shown, taking a swipe at the ends of the stems with my knife to even them out while still holding them in midair—I paused for a few seconds to look around the vast expanse of leafiness, all destined to feed fortunate, appreciative people, and felt that

Richard and Holley had gotten it exactly right. The very existence of their farm was lucky for everyone involved. I was somewhat giddy from exertion and hunger (not to mention caffeine deprivation), and an Emily Dickinson poem I had memorized in college popped into my mind:

> A little Madness in the Spring
> Is wholesome even for the King
> But God be with the Clown—
> Who ponders this tremendous scene—
> This whole Experiment of Green—
> As if it were his own!

It wasn't spring, but I surely resembled a clown in my oversized, mud-smeared plastic pants, wielding a knife and surveying the acreage around me. This farm had fed me in the past and would again in the future, and I felt, at that moment, that it was at least a tiny bit mine.

This feeling got me through another hour of cutting kale and then rainbow chard—great plumes of green with bright orange, yellow, fuchsia, and red stems at their centers, which we chopped and bound into bunches like the kale (though the plants were much taller so there was, thankfully, no squatting). Then it was time to climb back into the trucks, which we had loaded with our many, many crates, and return to the barn. I had no idea what time it was, but the sun had only just risen fully above the hills behind the fields. I couldn't remember the last time I'd felt so productive this early in the day (scattering Cheerios across the kitchen floor,

I now realized, didn't really count), but all the same, I was freezing and thrilled to get back into the truck.

Back inside the barn (a roof! luxury!), the crew unloaded crates of lettuce and Ashley began to dump the heads into black plastic troughs filled with water. She agitated them for a few minutes to loosen the dirt, then grabbed a dripping lettuce in each hand and handed them to Micah, who shook them a little and put them into white cardboard boxes we had assembled, marked with Lucky Dog stickers on which we wrote the variety of lettuce each box held. This was repeated over and over, until the one thousand fifty-six lettuces were all washed and boxed. Then Ashley moved on to the baby spinach, which was packed loose in plastic bags in three-pound boxes.

Meanwhile Val, Alese, and I were back at the bean sorter, this time grabbing green and yellow beans. With thirty-two crates of twenty-five pounds each to get through—thousands and thousands of beans—the task seemed endless. And yet, compared with being out in a wet field, it was heaven. Somewhere around the twentieth crate, Val turned to me wild-eyed and said, "This makes you feel like you could go insane." And while I agreed with her wholeheartedly, I was also starting to enjoy myself. I had survived the frozen fields, the swinging knife, the coffeeless morning. Soon it would be time for lunch.

The midday meal ended up being a hurried affair in the hoop house attached to the office. The food was prepared by the mother of Alese, Kalan, Daniele, and Ashley, who came to the farm every day with Alese and Micah's three-year-old daughter, a little blond imp who had popped into the barn while we were sorting beans. But hurried didn't mean bad. There were deviled farm eggs, tuna sandwiches on Holley's bread, pickles, and a few other things I can't remember because I was too busy cramming them into my mouth with delight. We were going to embark on the muddy potato harvest that afternoon, and I wanted to be well fueled for it.

After eating we went back out to the fields, to another patch of kale (there were eleven crates of it still to pick), which was next to a patch of collard greens. By this time the day was so warm that we shed our plastic pants and headed into the rows of collards and kale in t-shirts, jeans, and boots. I was sweating as I cut huge fanlike fronds off the collard plants, which were about three feet tall and resembled miniature palm trees, then banded them with tags and put them into crates. The afternoon was flying by, and Holley came out of the store to help us cut so that we wouldn't be any later with the produce order than we absolutely had to be.

After the kale and collards, we were off to the potato field, row after row of them grown from seed potatoes planted into ridges of soil the previous spring. Richard had prepared for the harvest by running a potato digger, pulled by a tractor, over the field. The digger had turned over the soil and torn the potatoes from their vines; now our job was to dig them out of the dirt. (Larger potato farms use a harvesting machine that digs the potatoes, sorts them, and loads them into boxes, thereby avoiding the need for manual labor.) Facing the long rows, I could see some potatoes scattered on top of the dirt, but most of them were underground. The only way to get at them was to straddle a row on your knees and claw at the soil with your hands.

"The thing is not to be afraid to get your pants dirty," Micah told me as he shuffled along a row on his knees, digging away. Down I went. From the first two feet of my row, I dug up about a dozen fingerling potatoes—the variety was called Russian Banana—which were a pale beige-yellow with translucent skin. The digging was like being at the beach as a kid, playing in the sand, and as I got into the spirit of it, I let go of any effort to keep even semi-clean. My nails were filthy and I kept wiping sweat off my face only to replace it with dirt, but the sun was shining and my crate seemed to fill quickly (potatoes, even small ones, are a lot bigger than spinach leaves).

But then I dug my hand down into the most disgusting substance I've ever seen or smelled. It turns out that rotten potatoes under the soil decompose into something that has the color and consistency of cottage cheese and smells like garbage that's been left in the sun. Now this scent and the goo that produced it were all over my right hand. Looking at me from the next row, Holley said sympathetically, "I like to use a rock," and demonstrated, taking off the top layer of soil with a wide, flat stone so she could check for potato rot before digging with her bare hands. Wiping the muck onto my jeans—they were a mess anyway by this time—and adopting this method with a rock I searched out at the edge of the field, I moved up my row as fast as I could. The Angello's Distributing truck had arrived half an hour before, and now

I could see its driver coming across the field to help us dig. If he didn't get back on the road more or less on schedule to drop off the truckful of produce at the warehouse, he would get even fewer than his usual five hours of sleep.

Up and down the rows we all went, digging, throwing potatoes into crates, hoisting full crates onto the truck parked on an unplanted section of the field. We had to come up with seven hundred pounds of potatoes. Hot and sweaty digging in the furrows, I found it hard to believe that a few hours earlier, which now seemed like a thousand years ago, I'd been freezing cold and longing for a hat. My arms were tired from carrying crates around and cutting and digging. My legs hurt from squatting and shuffling. I was in awe of the others, who did this on a daily basis.

At last the digging was done, and we all walked back to the barn for what turned out to be one more episode of *I Love Lucy*. While half the crew started loading the Angello's truck with the boxes of produce, Alese, Val, Ashley, and I parked ourselves by the potato washer. The minute I saw the conveyor belt, I knew what was coming. At one end of the machine was a long water-filled trough that, after Micah dumped several crates of the newly dug fingerlings into it, became a kind of potato river. After soaking for a minute, the potatoes were pushed through the machine, which sprayed them with water, then brushed them, then sent them across a row of sponges to remove some of the water before dropping them onto a circular conveyor belt. We were stationed, as at the bean sorter, on both sides of the belt to pick out both potatoes with signs of rot (nothing so vile as in the field, fortunately) and very small ones, called "peanuts," which were set aside for sale in the farm store.

The catch this time was that we had to take all the potatoes off the belt, even the good ones, and throw them into different crates at our sides. Peanuts, left. Bad ones, right. Perfect specimens, left, but lower down. The pressure was exacerbated by the speed at which the crates were being removed—as fast as we could fill them—in order to get the potatoes into boxes and onto the waiting truck. I had roasted, peeled, and sliced these potatoes many times at applewood, and never once had it occurred to me that people had sorted them by hand after crawling around in the dirt to harvest them. I had noticed that the potatoes were delicious, something I attributed in part to the fact that they had not been out of the ground very long or traveled very far to reach the kitchen, but I had never thought about what had happened to make that short trip between farm and kitchen possible.

Finally the Angello's driver closed the back of his truck and drove off, and my fellow workers began to leave for home. I looked up at the clock, expecting to see that it was at least seven in the evening. It was five-twenty. As the crew disbanded, Richard and I walked up to the house, where we found Asa waiting at the back door. Sweeping his son into his arms, Richard grinned at me and said, "I wasn't sure you were going to work, but I'm sure glad you did." It was the only sign I had seen all day that he had been strained by the enormous order and the incredible effort to get it together in time for everyone to go home at a decent hour. He was used to it, after all. Even though we had harvested more than usual, the rhythm of the day had been more or less typical of a busy Wednesday at Lucky Dog.

Driving back down to the city (something I really shouldn't have done considering how tired I was, but being around Asa and Sybilla had made me miss Jules), I couldn't stop thinking about how much food we'd harvested in a single day, how hard we had worked, and yet how good I felt. "There is work that is isolating, harsh, destructive, specialized or trivialized into meaninglessness," Wendell Berry wrote in his essay "The Body and the Earth." "And there is work that is restorative, convivial, dignified and dignifying, and pleasing. Good work is not just the maintenance of connections—as one is now said to work 'for a living' or 'to support a family'—but the *enactment* of connections. It *is* living, and a way of living; it is not support for a family in the sense of an exterior brace or prop, but is one of the forms and acts of love."

This second type of work was what I had been doing, and what Berry said made perfect sense to me. After you've been digging in a potato field and eaten eggs from the henhouse next to the farmhouse you're sitting in, food seems, if only temporarily, very simple; so does supporting people who grow it carefully. And supporting them didn't mean I had to forgo the occasional bag of non-local carrots, which I bought when I had to because carrots were one of the few things Jules would eat. It meant making the right choice as often as possible, and accepting that that was all any of us could do. "I'd like us all to talk not about denying ourselves but about making changes," Richard had said at the weed pile the day before. "We have to make an investment in what we think is true."

❖

The day after I returned from Lucky Dog was a Thursday, when produce deliveries came to the restaurant. When I got there, the bounty waiting to be put away in the walk-in included seven boxes from Lucky Dog, the very ones I had helped fill just twelve hours earlier. Even this recently removed from the farm, the food looked entirely different. In the muddy barn, the potatoes and spinach and lettuces had seemed part of a natural cycle of work, weather, and consumption. Here, they just looked like vegetables.

I carried a box of spinach upstairs to the kitchen. Opening it, I flashed back to the cold, wet field, the number of swipes I'd made with my knife to fill a single crate (the box probably held a crate and a half's worth of leaves). I almost wanted to beg for mercy for the spinach. On some level, it seemed wrong to use up something I'd worked so hard to harvest. But of course, the work that happens on a farm is not the end, but the means to the real end, which is eating. As Wendell Berry put it, "Eating ends the annual drama of the food economy that begins with planting and birth."

As I was indulging in my philosophical reverie, David passed by, peered into the box, grabbed a few stems to munch, and asked, "Did you pick these?" When I nodded, he lit up. "Awesome!" Then he was gone, leaving me and Liza to devise a use for the spinach. "Since you picked it, you should cook it," she said as I continued to gaze into the box as though cooking and serving the baby leaves would be like killing a litter of puppies. "Creamed spinach," she said briskly. "Destem it and then I'll show you what to do."

For the next forty-five minutes I stood by the box of spinach, taking out leaves one at a time and snapping off their stems before tossing them into a fish box. (Like many things in the kitchen, these low, rectangular plastic containers, called fish boxes because their tight-fitting lids made them ideal for storing raw fish in the walk-in, also served other purposes. This one made a perfect temporary holding tank for my spinach leaves.) With each snap, I turned and threw the stem into a nearby garbage can, until Liza caught sight of what I was doing. She came over with a quart container, which she wedged into a corner of the spinach box. "You're wasting a lot of time turning to the trash can," she said, somehow managing not to sound annoyed. "It's all about efficiency." Then she showed me how to save precious seconds by just dropping the stems into the quart container. Suddenly I had new insight into all the times Noah and I had thrown a dinner party and found ourselves chopping and sautéing and boiling—and arguing about why we were still doing it—at the very last second.

Box of destemmed spinach in hand, I went to Liza for further instructions. "First we're going to make a béchamel sauce," she said. "Go get an onion, and put a fine dice on it." I did this and threw the onion into a pan of butter to sweat. ("This restaurant is not about nutrition," Liza told me more than once as we heedlessly pitched hunks of butter, which David bought in one-pound blocks, into pans. She meant that it wasn't about low-fat or "healthy" eating in the sense of dieting, though I'm sure there are more vitamins in a serving of Lucky Dog spinach straight from the farm than there are in many processed foods people eat in their quest to be healthy.) There was no room on the stove—a gigantic pot of something with apples floating in it was taking up three burners, and there were various other pans, including the ever-present pot of blanching water for prep—so we put the onion pan on the grill.

When the onions were translucent but not brown, I added enough flour to absorb the butter and the onion juices and cooked away the raw flour taste to make a roux. Then I added cream to make it into a sauce.

With the béchamel done, I heated canola oil in a frying pan, then tossed in handfuls of spinach and some salt and left them there for just a few seconds, until the leaves were wilted. I was supposed to flip them, but the pan was heavy and I was far too chicken to attempt the casual, one-handed toss everyone else in the kitchen executed a thousand times a day. Instead of flipping I stirred, and in the stirring, lost some of the leaves as the spoon pushed them out of the pan. Within seconds my pan was surrounded by pieces of flaming spinach that had landed on burners that were turned on but not currently in use. Each one flared briefly and disappeared, all my hard work turned to ashes. The only thing worse than cooking the spinach you had picked by hand in the chill and dark for people to eat, I discovered, was incinerating it purposelessly.

Finally all the spinach was sautéed (ratio of vaporized leaves to properly cooked ones, approximately three to twenty). We let it cool in a stainless steel pan and then chopped it up and put it in quart containers. To serve it, we threw a handful in a pot with béchamel sauce, heated it all up, and put it in a ramekin. When I tasted my first bite, it was redolent not only with the smooth flavor of butter and the earthy, mineral taste of the spinach, but also with memories of those green fields upstate. In that moment I felt as near to the earth as I had while cutting the baby leaves the day before.

The following week when I arrived for work, David strode out into the dining room to meet me, wiping his hands on his apron, before I made it back to the kitchen.

"One of Richard's farmhands was killed," he said, emotion rising in his voice. "It was the husband of this woman," he said, pointing to one of the black-and-white photographs of the farm displayed on the restaurant walls. The photo showed Alese, hair up, in cut-offs, boots, and a bikini top, holding heads of lettuce in the middle of a field.

Micah.

"Did you work with him?" David asked.

"Yes." I thought of the potato fields and his little daughter wandering around the barn while I packed produce with her mother.

Micah had died in a car accident that weekend, I learned from the obituary Laura taped up on the kitchen wall. By dinner service that night, Laura and David had decided to put an insert in the check folders telling diners what had happened and how Micah was connected to the restaurant and asking for support for his family, soon to expand by one. Unsurprisingly, the most donations came from customers seated at the table under Alese's picture.

Her second baby, born in early April of the following year, six months after its father's death, was a boy. She named him Micah.

❖ Lucky Dog Creamed Spinach

1½ pounds fresh spinach
2 onions
½ pound butter
1 cup flour
2 cups heavy cream
2 tablespoons canola oil
salt

1. Destem the spinach and fine-dice the onions.
2. Sweat the onions in butter in a deep sauté pan over low heat.
3. When the mixture has reduced enough so there is still some liquid but no color on the onions, add the flour and stir until the butter and onion juices are absorbed.
4. Cook about 15 minutes until flour loses raw taste, then add the cream.
5. While the béchamel sauce cooks, heat the canola oil in a sauté pan and toss the spinach in the oil with salt, very quickly, to wilt it.
6. Chop the spinach and mix with the sauce to serve.

Serves 4 as a side.

7

❖

Into the Frying Pan

YOU MAY BE WONDERING at this point how things
were going in my own dining room. The answer is badly.
Jules had consumed no cheese (apparently my new understanding of what it was had not improved my powers of per-
suasion). Also no meat, and definitely no pasta (though he
had deigned to touch a piece once, picking it up and exam-
ining it thoughtfully, as if studying an ancient relic, before
calmly putting it back on his plate without a word). We had,
however, scored a major victory on the toast front. By starting him off with raisin bread, we had finally managed to persuade him first to eat it toasted, absolutely dry, and then to
eat it as French toast (which counted as a double victory since
he refused to eat eggs in any other configuration—slathering
them in syrup, for some reason, seemed to win him over).

I stand before you now as a person who never in her
wildest dreams thought she'd be offering secret thanks to a
higher power just because her child was willing to eat bread,

and yet that is exactly what I did. My thanks were secret because Noah and I had stopped saying anything congratulatory to Jules when he was eating for fear that the very idea that we liked what he was doing would cause him to stop. I was so delighted that we could finally take Jules out to dinner and be assured that he would at least eat something out of the breadbasket that I chose to ignore his perverse habit of eating, unlike any other child I've ever known, only the crusts of his bread. On a weekend trip to Philadelphia around this time, he actually refused to eat a peanut butter and jelly sandwich (a meal we had come to rely on) brought to him by room service—under a fancy silver dome, no less—because it had the crusts cut off. He also turned down French fries. Yet somehow he was growing.

And so was I, in a different way. I had spent my first night "on fish" in the kitchen, and I had survived.

A night at the fish station—made up of one person, an oven, four to six burners depending on how many the grill chef needs, a lowboy fridge, and about two by three feet of stainless steel countertop—begins when the first handwritten yellow ticket comes in and gets stuck in front of you. The first few orders are easy. There's time to consider how to plate, to froth the soup a little bit longer (soup is the fish station's responsibility), to sauté a stray piece of fish for the rest of the chefs. But once the servers start dashing in and firing tables at a steady pace, usually around seven-thirty to eight o'clock, just as the first rush at garde manger is slowing, the rest of the night flies by in a haze of spattering oil, burning-hot pots and pans, dirty side towels, sweat, sauces, reductions, quarts of water, jokes with the other chefs, panic when the board is full of tickets with nothing but fish orders on them, forgotten orders of soup that you have to heat instantly while you're juggling three frying pans and six other pots, adrenaline, shouted orders to the chef on grill, who can't see the tickets — "You're ordered in on a duck and two veal! You have three ducks all day!" (meaning three orders of duck in total) — and a thousand other tiny details you're too busy to notice until dinner service is over and you realize you've consumed at least six desserts' worth of cookies and about twenty pieces of bread over the course of the night. (I could never figure out if I ate more when I was busy or when I was bored, but either way, I gained ten pounds during my year at the restaurant.)

But as I put on my chef's jacket for my first night on fish, I didn't yet know about any of this.

From the safety of my spot at garde manger, everything seemed to move like clockwork over at the fish station, even on a busy night. There was the occasional blip, but even if orders did get backed up, David, who often worked the fish station because from its central location he could manage both the cooking and the expediting of food out to the dining room, just kept moving forward. It looked like fun, actually, and later — much later — I would get to the point where it was. But not until my literal baptism by fire was long behind me.

The fish menu that first night had three appetizers, two soups, and four entrées. I started my shift confidently, with David watching over me and somehow managing to look genuinely curious about what I might be able to pull off rather than regretful of his offer to let me try it out. I had proven myself at garde manger as far as keeping things moving during the dinner rush went, but this was something else entirely. The kitchen even looked different from in front of the stove, which was farther from the door and thus further down the rabbit hole than garde manger. I stood behind my counter, a stack of neatly folded green-and-white-striped side towels in front of me and one tucked into the tie of my apron, waiting.

At six-thirty the first ticket arrived, along with the server's look of surprise that I was the person there to receive it. A patron had come into the bar alone and ordered a bowl of lobster broth—a misnomer since the soup was made with a base of lobster stock, heavy cream, apples, fennel, onions, tomatoes, and brandy. This mixture, stored in quart containers, was waiting in the lowboy at the fish station.

I swung into action, scooping about three big spoonfuls of broth base into a pot and dousing it with heavy cream before setting it on the fire. "How long?" I asked David. "Until it's hot," he answered. (This was typical of his unintentional Zen riddle responses to questions involving precision. "How much?" was usually met with "Enough" or "More than you would ever think," which usually pertained to adding salt.) When the mixture was heated through, I pulled it off the burner and "zapped" it in the pot with a stick blender to combine the cream and base and make it frothy. Then I pulled a small, low bowl from the shelf above the stove where the serving dishes sat to stay warm and poured the soup into it over a spoon so that it wouldn't splash all over the bowl. I placed a small pile of chives in the center, and the order was ready to go. As David handed it to the server, I recalled that I had ordered the lobster broth the first time I ate at applewood. Even making it myself hadn't really removed the mystery of what made it so insanely delicious—it was as smooth as silk and tasted like the very essence of lobster—but I was at least one step closer.

When the next ticket came in, around six-forty-five, the top half read "lobster app," "red leaf (split)," and the bottom half said "scallops," "duck," and "gnocchi." While David yelled to Sarah, "You're ordered in on a duck and a gnocchi!" (he had wisely decided to do that part of the fish station's duties himself), I opened a quart of dayboat scallops from Cape Cod and placed three of them on the counter on a paper towel. Then I opened a quart of lobster pieces for the appetizer and put a tail, two claws, and a few knuckles into a small metal bowl and passed them to Sarah to toss on the grill. While they were getting color, I grabbed two radishes and a mandoline (eek!) and sliced the red globes into another small metal bowl, to which I added olive oil, chives, salt, and lemon juice. Next I set up a small sauce pot with the scallop sides I had prepped in the afternoon—roasted cipollini onions, blanched baby carrots, a handful of pea shoots, salt, and a dollop of butter—and placed it on a low burner so it would be ready for a final blast of heat when it was time to fire the dish.

When the lobster came back to me, nicely marked by the grill—"Your lobster, Madame!"—I put on a plastic glove, tossed the radish salad with my fingers, then heaped it in the middle of a bright yellow plate.

"Let's see if we can kind of pile the lobster on," David said. He had never made this appetizer before, so he was working out how the plate should look as he went along (which of course brought to mind, and then crushed, the old adage about never cooking something for the first time when you have dinner guests coming).

We stacked the lobster pieces on top of the radish slices, trying to curve the claws around so they wouldn't fall off, adjusting them until finally they all seemed stable. With a fast pinch, David grabbed one knuckle out of the pile and placed it on the other side for visual balance, then took the quart of pesto I was holding out to him and said, "Let's make a quenelle."

Plunging a large spoon into the pesto, he brought it sideways against the container and dragged a spoonful of pesto up to the lip so that it took on the shape of an egg that had been flattened on one side. He repeated this motion a few more times, shaping the pesto into a fat cylinder with a ridge on the top, about an inch and a half long, then very carefully deposited it on the lobster plate, with one edge on the radish salad. It was a beautiful fresh, mossy green against the pale salad dotted with chives, and the red edges of the radish disks were mirrored in the color of the lobster.

"Perfect!" he said. "Great job." Then he handed the plate to the extern working garde manger that night, who put it down on the counter closest to the door, next to the red leaf salad with pickled nectarines, sorrel, and red wine vinaigrette that he had made and neatly divided onto two plates. Then he stuck his head several inches out into the dining room and called "Pick up!" One of the servers came and took the plates, and my hard-won inaugural appetizer was gone. My first thought was that I'd never have another chance to make that lobster appetizer for that person.

On the other hand, I had done almost nothing—Sarah had grilled, David had mostly stacked—and though I had made the pesto during prep, forming it into a quenelle seemed hopelessly out of my reach (apparently there was another method for doing it that used two spoons and required transferring the pesto back and forth between them instead of using the side of a quart, but that sounded even harder). And yet David was as encouraging as if I'd just worked a shift alone. "How was that?" he asked enthusiastically.

I was about to reply when the door swung into the kitchen and Laura strode in, stopping in her tracks when she saw me standing behind the fish counter. She hadn't heard about my "promotion" (early on she had told me she often felt as if she and David worked at different restaurants since neither of them really knew what was going on in the other's part).

"Wow," she said, throwing David a look.

"Melanie's working fish!" he said in the voice I imagined he'd used to announce that Sophie had ridden her bike alone for the first time or that Tatum had eaten her first bite of duck confit.

"Wowww!" Laura said again, grinning at me this time. I guessed at what she was thinking: this might turn out to be misguided, but David was standing by to mop up any mess I made, and anyway, the fish station was his problem, not hers.

"You can fire those scallops," Sarah called from the grill. Meat had to be started before fish since it took longer and had to rest after grilling, so the fish station took its cues from the grill in order to send out whole orders at the same time.

"Okay!" I said, masking my fear with feigned exuberance.

I already had a black iron frying pan sitting on a lit burner, so I added some canola oil. ("How much?" I asked David. "You know," he said, "some.") While the oil was heating, I pulled the three waiting scallops off their paper towel and put them in my palm, held a box of fine sea salt up high with my other hand and rained salt down onto the scallops, then turned them over and salted the other side.

Before lifting the pan I grabbed a side towel—there was no such thing as a potholder in the kitchen, only side towels which you folded and used between your hand and the hot metal handles. I tipped the pan so that the oil rushed to the far edge, placed the scallops in it one by one, then tipped it level again and let the oil swirl around them with a satisfying sizzle. I turned up the fire under the pot I'd already filled with the pea shoots, onions, and carrots and turned to the counter, pleased with my performance so far. Over at the grill, Sarah was draining the fat off a duck breast and stirring her gnocchi, which she was serving with beet greens, caramelized onions, and toasted almonds as the vegetarian entrée.

"You can go ahead and plate," she said calmly.

I turned back to my scallops, looking to David for guidance.

"Get your plate ready and they'll be done," he said.

Grabbing a white plate off the hot shelf above the stove, I worried about getting the scallops out of the pan. David used a spoon for some reason, a technique I didn't ask about and definitely didn't dare try, but I wasn't sure what to do instead.

I set the plate on the counter and plated the cipollinis, baby carrots, and pea shoots. Then I stared at the scallops for a few seconds, dreading the next step.

"Okay. Grab your fish spatula," David told me, meaning *his* fish spatula. "Now slide it under one scallop."

I had never concentrated so hard in my life. The spatula stuck halfway under the scallop, which seemed unwilling to budge. I wiggled it as the other two scallops kept cooking, simultaneously humiliated that I couldn't get the first one out of the pan and convinced that the other two were going to be black.

"Try to do it in one swift motion," David said, taking the fish spatula from me and sliding it (needless to say, in one swift motion) under the scallop. Then he flipped the scallop, removed it immediately to the waiting plate, and laid it carefully on top of the vegetables.

Round two. This time the spatula didn't get stuck, but once the scallop was on the spatula, I couldn't figure out how to flip it. Finally I gave it a little toss and it landed in the pan on its side before falling into position. I could feel the clock ticking along with the pounding of my heart, and Sarah had already plated her duck and her gnocchi. There was a table of diners waiting for their food and I was holding it up.

When the second scallop was on the plate, I tried a third time. Because the pan now held just one lone scallop, I had no trouble getting the spatula under it and flipping it. I needed lots of space to move food around, the antithesis of efficient restaurant cooking.

I settled the final scallop onto the vegetables, and David grabbed a quart of red wine vinaigrette from the counter. With a spoon, he drizzled the vinaigrette over the scallops and around the vegetables, where it added a pleasing wine-dark contrast to the bright carrots and pea shoots and the golden scallop tops (I hadn't burned them after all).

"Pickup!" David yelled to no one in particular as the door swung open. And the order went out.

My brain was aching as I reviewed the details of making the lobster appetizer and the scallops so I'd remember for next time: when the order came in, you took the protein out of the lowboy, then you got the appetizers going, then you set up the sides for the entrées, then you fired your appetizers, making sure you were in tune with the grill if there were grill items on the ticket, then you fired your entrées, then you plated, and in the meantime, probably, four more tickets had come in so you were reaching for more fish and balancing more pots on the burners because there wasn't room for each one to have a burner to itself, and the metal stubs of stove knobs were hotter than ever.

"I think it's going to be slow tonight," David said cheerfully, "so it will be perfect for you."

❖

Of course it was not slow.

It was not slow the next time I had to flip scallops, and it was not slow the first or any time I had to assemble and then flip delicate crab cakes—grab a handful of crabmeat from a quart, mix it in a bowl with chives, egg, shallots, and other herbs, form two patties, throw them into a hot pan with a little bit of hot oil in it, plate with cucumber jalapeño salad and milk-poached garlic purée—which tended to fall apart at the touch of my spatula (one bowl, one pot). It was not slow when I had to grill pieces of cobia (a firm white fish)—stepping close to Sarah and laying them on an empty spot on the grill, then remembering to step back and flip them and then to step back again to remove them—and serve each one in a big bowl in a shallow pool of aromatic lobster stock called *nage* with baby bok choy and roasted shallots (two more pots). It was still not slow the first time I had to cook and plate grouper, which was started in a pan and finished in the oven, out of sight so I risked forgetting all about it, then served with collard greens and applewood smoked bacon sauce (one pan, one pot, one quart to dip into for sauce). Nor was it slow when three people ordered halibut, pan seared and served with celery root–cabbage slaw, mint pesto, and roasted garlic lemon aioli (one pan, three quarts). The kitchen was humming along by then, plates clattering into the busing tub when the servers brought them back from the dining room, the door swinging in and out, in and out, the pans sizzling, cries of "oven open" and "pickup" above the rushing-water sound of the dishwasher. Sarah was spinning around expertly, plating braised pork belly appetizers and duck with fingerling potatoes and rabbit with risotto and golden tomatoes. By this time I had three frying pans and seven pots going simultaneously—one soup, five pieces of fish, six sides including the lobster nage—and a huge line-up of fish on the counter waiting to be cooked. And I was starting to lose my grip.

"Is this halibut ready, do you think?" I asked David, wiping my drenched face with a side towel.

"What do you think?" he asked calmly, as though we were not surrounded by fire and sweat and there were no hungry people on the other side of the glass-paned door.

"I don't know!" I shrieked. "I'm a writer!"

As we both cracked up, I singed all the hair off my right arm reaching behind the halibut pan to a back burner for the pot of collard greens and bacon to go with the grouper I was about to take out of the oven.

But the halibut did not burn (later that week, when I scorched a piece of bass, David whisked the skin off it in one quick motion, gave me a mischievous look, and said "They'll never know!"). In fact, nothing was burned but the hair on my arm and, into my brain, the phantom image of many, many pieces of cobia lined up on the grill long after the dinner rush was over.

There was a fluke carpaccio appetizer, with brown butter croutons made to order and lemon parsley gremolata, that I never even attempted to make or plate. David was on fluke. There was also a thirty-minute period when I just slid away from the stove, leaving six pots and four frying pans going and begging for mercy while he took over with an easy, "I'll just get us through this next part." When I went back to the burners, he plated for me so I could catch my breath.

By the end of the night I was mildly humiliated even though I knew perfectly well that no one expected me to be able to do anything. Walking the two blocks home, I felt as if everything I'd learned in the previous months added up to nothing when it came to actually cooking a meal.

Then again, there were those irritating crab cakes, of which I made thirty that night. By the time I got to the final two I thought I had the hang of it—the mixing, the molding, the flipping—but at the last minute, watching them sizzle in the pan, I lost my nerve.

"They're going to break," I half-screeched to David.

"They do break," he said by way of encouragement, and it was true, I'd seen him break a few himself. But still, my pride was on the line.

"Well," I said, "I'd rather you break them than I break them. It's your restaurant."

He gave me a look. "Go ahead. Just do it."

Exhausted, drenched with sweat, wielding a fish spatula ferociously, I flipped them—one, two. And the restaurant, just for those seconds, became, for the first time, a little bit mine, too. I couldn't handle fish on my own, but with David there I had done okay. I was only half a chef, but then again, that was half more than I'd been at six-thirty that night, back when that first ticket had rolled in.

❖ Easy Flip Raisin French Toast

2 eggs
½ cup milk
cinnamon to taste
3 tablespoons butter
4 slices raisin bread

1. In a low dish, scramble the eggs, milk, and cinnamon.

2. Heat the butter over medium heat in a heavy frying pan big enough to hold all the slices at once. When the butter is melted, tip the pan to make it cover the entire bottom.

3. One by one, dip pieces of bread in the egg mixture, flipping each one to make sure it absorbs egg on both sides and all the way through. Place them in the buttered pan and leave them, untouched, for 2–3 minutes or until they have browned nicely.

4. Flip each slice and fry the other side for an additional 2–3 minutes.

5. Serve with maple syrup.

Serves 2 hungry adults or 4 kids for breakfast.

❖ Not So Easy Flip Crab Cakes

1 pound fresh crabmeat
2 eggs
3 shallots, minced

½ cup minced chives, plus any additional herbs you
    want to add (tarragon, chervil, and parsley are good
    ones)
3 tablespoons canola oil

1. Clean the crabmeat thoroughly, sorting it piece by piece to remove any remaining cartilage or shell (even if you're buying it pre-cleaned, it's important to do this).

2. In a metal bowl, combine the crabmeat, eggs, shallots, chives, and other herbs (by hand is best, though you can use a rubber spatula or a spoon).

3. Heat the canola oil in a heavy pan over medium heat. When the oil is hot, take small handfuls of the crab mixture and form patties about 2½–3 inches across (any bigger and you'll never get them flipped).

4. Place the patties in the oil—I recommend just 2 at a time so you have space to get the spatula into the pan—and let them cook for about 5 minutes.

5. When they are golden brown on the first side, slide your spatula under each one and flip it in one swift motion. Go ahead. Just do it.

6. Cook the patties on the second side for an additional 5 minutes or so, then remove to a plate and keep warm while you cook the rest of the mixture.

Serves 4 as an appetizer.

8

❖

One Fish, Two Fish

THE FIRST WEEKEND Noah and I spent together, he made pasta with puttanesca sauce—black olives, capers, garlic, anchovies, and a dash of hot red pepper. He also made tea for me one cold afternoon as the light was fading behind the snowy hills outside his house. What struck me was not so much the tea itself as the fact that he had a teapot, which I did not, and which, it seemed to me, meant that he was generous and knew how to gather people around him and take care of them. I didn't think consciously about any of this until much later, but the teapot stuck in my mind for many months, until I had spent enough time with him to see that my interpretation of it had been right. There are few activities Noah loves more than to feed people. He's an instinctive cook, one who never uses recipes and who can, if nothing else is available, whip up a plate of leftovers for dinner that turns a makeshift meal into a banquet. He swears by the principle that cracking an egg over just about anything you happen to have turns it into a delicious dish, which turns out to be true roughly ninety percent of the time. There are some things even an egg can't save.

That puttanesca was my first lesson in the differences between us. The first meal I ever made for Noah was duck breasts (I bought them already butchered, obviously) with raspberry sauce from a recipe—a very long one—I had cut out of a magazine. I remember clearly every step of making it, from spending practically my entire weekly paycheck on the duck, a food I had never cooked before, to panicking my way through the recipe while Noah was out having drinks with a friend because I was too nervous to have him in the kitchen with me. In the end, it was satisfying in a complicated, showy way—everything Noah's pasta had not been. He wanted to feed me, and I wanted a challenge.

This was pretty much how things remained in our relationship when it came to food. Along the way, we got married, I taught myself how to cook insanely elaborate Indian food out of a book, we had Jules, and Noah started inventing cocktails (sometimes out of necessity—the apex of his improvisational skills came when he served the wife of a colleague a cosmo made with a pale pink juice I didn't recognize and, after she proclaimed it delicious, told her it was fruit punch from one of Jules's juice boxes). Pasta, large pieces of meat, and salads were Noah's domain. I was in charge of smaller pieces of meat, whole chickens (or any chicken), plus fish and any other weird recipe I cut out of the newspaper or found in a cookbook and wanted to try. Which was how we ended up surmounting one of our toughest challenges to date with our friends David (not Shea, but one of the most appreciative eaters I've ever met) and Steve (one of the best cooks I've ever met).

We had been introduced to Steve and David just before Jules came along, and the four of us started having dinner frequently, never out, always in. One night at their apartment, about six months after I'd started cooking at applewood, we got into a discussion of the minutiae of kitchen work. By the time it was over, Steve and I had decided we needed to plan a blow-out cooking event involving some over-the-top meal neither of us would have the guts to tackle on our own. Had I not made so many errors and enjoyed my few small triumphs at the restaurant, had I not become accustomed to doing idiotic things in front of people who could really cook, I'm not sure I would ever have agreed to this. But I had come some distance in the last months—if nothing else I had learned how to fail and move on in the kitchen—and I was game.

A date was set. A recipe was chosen. The four of us gathered at five P.M. to allow plenty of time for mishaps. Steve and I had chosen Lobster à l'Américaine, misleadingly described simply as "lobster simmered with wine, tomatoes, garlic, and herbs" in Julia Child's *Mastering the Art of French Cooking.*

I received my copy of this book from my mother on the occasion of my successful execution of Julia's Veal Prince Orloff, a recipe I took from *her* copy. Veal Prince Orloff involves (I'm just going on memory here) about a thousand different sauces and fillings, plus the roasting, slicing, reconstruction, saucing, and re-baking of a very large veal roast so that it looks as if you've never taken a knife to it. It's the kind of recipe, according to Julia, designed for "the servant-less American cook who can be unconcerned on occasion with budgets, waistlines, time schedules, children's meals, the parent-chauffeur–den mother syndrome, or anything else which might interfere with the enjoyment of producing something wonderful to eat."

Lobster à l'Américaine was also this kind of recipe, so I felt lucky that we were not only servantless and all those other things, but also profoundly unconcerned with Jules's meal because he didn't really want one. Instead, he ate yogurt while Steve and I pondered the torturously long recipe and Noah and David mixed some drinks. We had to cut up the lobsters, clean out their innards, crack the claws, sauté all the meat in its shell, dice carrots, onions, shallots, and garlic, put the vegetables in the pan with the lobster, set the whole mixture on fire with some cognac (whoopee!), add numerous other ingredients, simmer it all, then put it in the oven, take it out, reduce it, add the innards and butter to the pan, simmer it some more, and on and on. Eventually, after all the prep and the cooking, we were supposed to arrange the pieces on a platter and serve them with rice, the making of which sounded mercifully easy, even in Julia's words.

Where once I might have found just reading this recipe daunting, I now felt eager to start. I had learned to move swiftly through prep work and had seen the results of doing it well night after night at applewood. As for the lobsters themselves, I was emboldened by my night at the fish station. Steve and David had arrived with three live ones that were waiting in a paper bag in our refrigerator. Before we could do any of that cracking, sautéing, or simmering, we had to kill them. I had never done this any other way besides throwing them into a pot of boiling water, but now I looked to Madame Child, who suggested that we "plunge the point of a knife into the head between the eyes, or sever the spinal cord by making a small incision in the back of the shell at the juncture of the chest and the tail." Steve and I rolled up our sleeves and set to work.

Except that once we had those lobsters out of the bag, neither of us could bear to stick a knife into their heads. (This was years before the movie *Julie & Julia* catapulted *MtAoFC* to the top of the bestseller list, but I'm guessing that about ninety-nine percent of the people who bought the book in an excited frenzy after seeing it, determined to cook like Julia, found themselves feeling the same way we did about adapting her lobster-killing method.) The doomed creatures scrabbled around on the kitchen counter as Jules watched curiously and Steve and I squealed and grabbed each other. We tried not to let Noah and David, lounging in the living room with their dry martinis, hear us, but eventually they wandered in to see what the problem was, at which point David immediately took himself off the list of possible lobster killers. He was far too gentle a soul for such considerations, he insisted, and none of us could disagree.

That left Noah.

About five years into our marriage, I had realized that one of the primary reasons to have dinner with friends is to learn things about your spouse that would never come up if the two of you were alone. Sometimes it's a political opinion, or a movie preference, or, as once happened to Noah, the discovery that your wife played the part of Rizzo in a summer-camp production of *Grease*. Sometimes it's the revelation that your husband is a practiced, cold-hearted murderer of crustaceans.

Noah talks often about his childhood—the sun, the surf, the sand—and had mentioned a few times that he had done a lot of spearfishing. It turned out this had given him a way with thrashing sea life. Now he stepped in for, literally, the kill.

Putting the three lobsters in our kitchen sink (thankfully deep enough to shield them from view), he picked up a butcher knife. I do not know what, exactly, happened next—though I suspect it was a little less elegant than Julia's method—because I was too busy jumping up and down and squealing with my hands over my ears to pay any attention. But moments later the lobsters were dead and Noah was telling me to stop making so much noise because I was going to scare Jules.

From there on out, things went smoothly. Noah put Jules to bed—no doubt to dream of claws—while Steve and I sweated and slaved and generally enjoyed ourselves. Every once in a while, as we diced and cracked and got spattered by the contents of the frying pan on the stove, we turned to each other, wiping our brows with dish towels (I longed for some side towels from the restaurant), and asked "Are you okay?" Then we would tackle the next step. To me it was not unlike being at applewood—the heat, the camaraderie, the mutual support. By the time we set our lobster pieces on our platter of rice and carried it to the table, I felt as if we'd been in a foxhole together. The food was amazing, and as the four of us sat around the table chewing and emitting little moans of happiness, David, Steve, and I laughed about our cowardice and toasted Noah. When the evening was over, figuring that Lobster à l'Américaine is the kind of dish you make only once in your life, or at least only once a decade, I didn't give my inability to stab lobsters between the eyes another thought.

That is, not until a crisp Thursday afternoon a few months later, when I arrived at applewood and Liza pointed to a box in the sink at the back of the room and casually uttered five words: "Want to kill some lobsters?"

Clearly this was no place for squealing and jumping. And though I was feeling fairly comfortable in the kitchen by then, I was still insecure enough to want to appear much more at home than I felt, so there would be no passing the buck, either.

"Just kill them by putting a knife in the head?" I asked, my voice squeaking as I tried to sound like a person not utterly reliant on my surfer husband to handle all crustacean emergencies.

"I usually just rip them apart with my bare hands," Liza said. I studied her face for a few seconds to see if she was joking, but I didn't see even the faintest hint of a smile.

I laughed anyway, probably because realizing she was serious made me nervous, and she gave me the odd look I deserved. Then I went to the back of the kitchen, looked at the dozen squirming lobsters in their wet box, put on a pair of rubber gloves, and tore them apart.

First I ripped off their claws, then their tails. The tails thrashed after they were removed, flexing back and forth as the nerves shuddered to a stop. The antennae on the heads twitched. And I did nothing. I didn't jump, or squeal, or even feel bad. Instead, I set aside the bodies for later use and took the oblong stainless steel pan I had placed the tails and claws in (called a hotel pan for reasons I never did figure out) to Liza, who dumped them in a pot of boiling water on the stove.

Something had happened to me while I wasn't paying attention. I had found peace and solace in chopping two crates of parsnips or shelling ten pounds of peas, tasks I would previously have considered tiresome, and now I had found a boldness (or maybe a viciousness) in the kitchen that surprised me. The learning curve, at least the first one, was flattening out.

Which was why, when David asked me at five that afternoon if I wanted to work fish again, I said yes, and then kept saying yes. I had developed a moderate case of the kind of cockiness Bill Buford suffered from just before getting temporarily fired—demoted to "the salt-and-pepper guy," no less—from the line at Babbo for cooking two pieces of meat incorrectly.

I spent the next few weeks at the fish station, which became my regular post, and while I was never threatened with firing—this being applewood, not Babbo, and David being

David rather than Mario Batali, facts for which I was unend-
ingly grateful—I felt as if I was going backwards. The more
I thought I knew, the less I was actually able to do. No matter what I remembered from one night to the next, I always
forgot something else: to add salt, to add stock instead of
water, how many gnocchi were in an appetizer. One night I
consistently had the flame too high under the fish pans; the
next night I got that flame right but let numerous pots of
sides go dry on the stove. I forgot to warm soup four times
in one night, then batted a thousand on soup the next night
while repeatedly forgetting to warm up the nage for a sea
bass dish (same basic process, different liquid, so what was
my problem?).

After David showed me how to press down on pieces of
fish with skin after putting them in the pan because otherwise the protein seized up and made the fish buckle, which
prevented the skin from crisping, I remembered to do it with
the bass but never the arctic char, the snapper, or anything
else. I forgot things during dinner service and during prep,
too. Once, after taking a few weeks off to write, I was making an ice bath in a big metal bowl for cooling blanched vegetables so they wouldn't lose their color, something we did
almost every day. I went downstairs to the ice machine and
filled the bowl with ice, then carried it back to the kitchen
and stood looking at it idiotically, trying to remember what
the second ingredient was, as moisture condensed on the
outside of the bowl and dripped onto my apron. Seeing my
blank expression, David took the bowl out of my hands and
half-filled it with water at the sink.

"You've been gone awhile, huh?" he said, laughing.

But apparently I was taking something in, because at home I was utterly relaxed in the kitchen. The night after my first stint at the fish station, I prepared dinner for four without blinking an eye: pasta carbonara, tomato salad with Lucky Dog tomatoes, and arugula salad. (Notice the happy absence of fish.) It had seemed ridiculously easy to cook for a measly four people who were all eating the same thing. Whereas once I would have consulted my recipe seven hundred times and worried about whether the egg yolks were going to cook too quickly when I poured them over the pasta, now I breezed ahead without any conscious thought at all. My knives, which I now sharpened every weekend, cut through the tomatoes with ease instead of sliding around and slicing into my skin as they had in the past.

Our tiny four-burner stove suddenly seemed profoundly manageable, producing in me a feeling of competence that grew stronger and stronger as the weeks passed. I got so bold I started burning myself at home almost as much as I did at the restaurant. I sizzled my hip on the edge of a pot and barely flinched. I pressed my fingers into smoking-hot pans to push fish down. I bought my own fish spatula and became obsessed with it. So light! So perfectly designed for its purpose! How had I ever lived without one? Because I had become accustomed to talking to David, who was generally no more than a foot from my side while I was on fish lest some mishap should befall me, I could now produce a fairly complicated meal while carrying on a conversation with dinner guests. I knew now that it was all in the prep work, and it seemed absurd that I had once had to banish Noah from the kitchen while I cooked. For every embarrassing night at applewood, I was enjoying a good one at home.

I didn't dare make any menu suggestions at work, but at the farmers' market on weekends, I was free to buy whatever appealed to me. Often I wished David were with me so I could ask him the kind of inane questions I asked on every shift — "Would this be good? How do I cook this? What can you do with this?" — but since he wasn't, I just started choosing produce and cuts of meat and pieces of fish and seeing what ideas came to me once I got them home.

Not everything I made was completely wonderful, but all of it was good. There were no disasters. And then, even as I continued to forget everything at the fish station at applewood, I made a string of meals at home that were not only seasonal and recipe-free but delicious. There was pork tenderloin with balsamic glaze served with kale and spaghetti squash. And there was chicken and dumplings, which my grandmother used to make from a recipe that had been lost to the ages and which I had been trying to re-create for years. When the flour on the chicken burned to the bottom of the pot, I had the sense to wash the pot and start over, substituting butter for the chicken fat I had been cooking with. When the dumplings were bobbing at the top of the pot, I took a bite and traveled right back to my grandmother's kitchen table.

My crowning achievement that week was a pasta with delicata squash, caramelized red onion, pine nuts, and sage. I had recently become addicted to delicata, a small, oblong, pale orange squash that has thin green stripes running its length and tastes a little like sweet potato. To cook it, you split it in half, scoop out the seeds, and roast it in the oven. You can eat the whole thing, including the skin, which gives any dish made with delicata a pleasing chewiness that other squash dishes often lack. Delicata is sturdy enough that Sarah sometimes served it as the vegetarian entrée, cut into angled cylinders and filled with bulgur salad or other grains or vegetables. I'd never heard of delicata before getting to applewood, and now, as with my fish spatula, I couldn't live without it.

The first time I roasted delicata at home, to make my improvised pasta dish, I was sure it wouldn't come out the same way it did at the restaurant, but it did. Then I caramelized some red onion in a pan with butter and tossed in pine nuts and shredded sage at the last minute. When it was done, I mixed everything from the pan, along with the diced squash, with fresh spaghetti from the Italian specialty store down the street. When I served it, Noah raised his eyebrows at me across the table and said, "I think all those shifts have started to pay off."

And then the culinary grace began to transfer. At work the day after the delicata pasta, I knew for the first time how to do everything David asked me to do. Perhaps most incredibly, I finally knew where everything was. When someone asked me for a hotel pan or a cutting board or a quart of cream, I handed it over with a "Here you go, Chef." I was still a novice at applewood, but I was sure of my place at last.

This feeling carried over to home, where I became picky about plating and what the garde manger book had called "presenting foods to look their best." I wiped microscopic specks of sauce off plates, and if food looked less perfect on the plate than it did at applewood, it jarred my senses. I was developing, as every good chef does, an ego about my kitchen.

One day I returned from some errands with a few tubes of mints to put in a little silver box that had been sitting empty on the runner on our dining room table for years. When Noah caught me in the act, he looked almost annoyed.

"This isn't a restaurant, you know," he said.

"I know . . . ," I trailed off, trying to give him a fierce look as I scuttled back to the kitchen to check on my latest production.

Which was fish sticks.

Jules, who was heading rapidly toward two, was still holding out when it came to meat, fish, cheese, and pasta. I had tried so many different foods on him by this time that I was ready to give up; he wouldn't even go near classic kid foods. When we got together with friends and their children, Noah and I watched miserably while the other kids gobbled down pizza and Jules ran around the table completely unin-terested — even though every other parent at the party had assured us that once he saw the others eating he'd join in. On the one hand, I secretly loved it that he was impervious to peer pressure, but on the other, I wanted to scream at him, "It's *pizza!*"

To which he probably would have answered, "Mama! Pizza! Mmmm." That was his current comment about any-thing we put on his plate, spoken just before he refused to try it. His use of "Mmmmm" never ceased to get my hopes up and also never meant he was going to take a bite.

"Mama. Chicken! Mmmmmm!"

"Mama! Fish! Mmm."

"Mama! Pasta! Mmmmm."

Cashews were his new love. Still in the cocktail-party phase, he had decided to try them when some friends invited us over for drinks and to meet their new baby. After walking around the room naming every food he saw but wouldn't eat—cheese, olives, pita bread—he discovered a bowl of cashews on a side table and consumed them happily. Our friends couldn't believe he was eating cashews at all, much less as his main course. When I mentioned with false nonchalance that they were a good source of protein and confessed that he wouldn't even eat pasta, the new mother nursing her sweet little infant looked aghast and I thought, "Just wait."

When you're cooking for children who won't eat, the law of diminishing returns eventually kicks in. The harder you try to make something that will tempt them, the less likely they are to eat it. Or at least this was the case at our house. Jules did far better with raw vegetables and fruit and the occasional bagel with peanut butter than he did with anything I made for him. Noah and I had both been reduced to thinking more about nutrition than food at dinnertime; as long as he was getting protein, carbs, vitamins, and calcium, we considered our work done.

One afternoon, in a grocery store near our apartment, I wandered the aisles looking for new things he might eat.

Somehow I found myself in the baby food section, and seeing all those little glass jars lined up on the shelves made me deeply nostalgic for his infancy. I remembered with perfect clarity the morning we had first fed him solid food—jarred peas—and how much he had loved it. From then until he was about a year old, he had eaten whatever we offered him as long as it was out of a jar (he never touched a single purée I made myself), even the things he would no longer go near, such as baby food with bits of meat or pasta in it.

Back then I had looked forward to the days when the messes and dirty clothes and stained bibs would be gone, but now those days of firsts—first peas, first laughs, first bites of crackers, first crawls—seemed almost painfully sweet and so simple. I wouldn't have traded the walking, talking ball of fire I now lived with, and yet something was gone. I had blotted out Jules's early days, no doubt because they were tangled up with memories of my father's illness and death, but now, at last, I felt I could go back. And though I knew the hazy wash of memory was obscuring all the difficult parts of life with a newborn, I was, for the first time, able to see both where I'd come from and where I'd arrived.

Which was, among other things, to a place of deep schizophrenia about food that had me using my treasured fish spatula to flip fish sticks. We bought a brand made with sustainably caught fish, because if I wasn't going to actually cook for my child, I could at least keep my politics about me. "Don't feel bad about yourself," Laura had told me a few weeks earlier, when I lamented that Jules had eaten a single raw string bean for dinner the night before and confessed that I was so desperate for him to ingest something both warm and containing protein that I was tempted to give him fish sticks. She went on, "Someone needs to write a story about how chefs' kids eat chicken nuggets out of the box." (I happened to know that her kids also ate frozen fish bites made from sustainably caught fish, and that David sometimes made them tacos from a box kit filled with additives, all of which did make me feel better.)

Maybe keeping these truths in mind made me just the tiniest bit more relaxed than usual when, on the evening Noah chided me about the mints, I prepared a plate of fish sticks, carrots and hummus, and almonds for Jules. I set his plate on the table, along with plates of carrots and hummus for me and for Noah. We all sat down.

"Mama!" said Jules. "Fishies! Mmm!"

"Yeah!" I said. "How about one for Mama, one for Jules?"

"Or one for Papa, one for Jules?" echoed Noah. Suffice it to say that when we'd met, eleven years earlier, neither of us had imagined having this conversation even once, much less every day for over a week.

Jules picked up a carrot and munched it thoughtfully. Then he picked up a fish stick and, even though it was rectangular, made it "swim" along the edge of his placemat. It's great when your child starts to develop an imagination, except when he uses it as a stall tactic.

"Swimming!" he said cheerfully, putting it back on his plate and taking another carrot.

Noah and I eyed each other nervously. We had been eating Jules's untouched fish sticks all week, and I didn't think I could manage one more bite.

But then, after taking a slug of his milk, Jules turned to me and offered me a fish stick with the bright invitation, "Mama and Jules eat fish?" Sensing something unfamiliar in his tone, I took a bite as fast as I could.

And then he did.

And then he took another bite, and another, and over the next fifteen minutes, during which I had to leave the table at one point because I felt I might cry with relief, he ate two entire fish sticks, the rest of his carrots, and a huge pile of almonds. That I had had to eat dozens of fish sticks myself in the previous weeks seemed a small price to pay for this moment.

"Suddenly I understand," said Noah, as Jules got down from his chair, "why parents take such pleasure in seeing their children eat. It's so elemental." He looked a little weepy, too.

The next day, talking to my sister on the phone, I admitted that perhaps I was overreacting to this not very unusual development. After all, most people's children had tried fish sticks and even real food as soon as they could chew.

"I feel like he just graduated from college or something," I confessed, slightly embarrassed.

"Well," she observed sagely, "it's kind of the same thing when you're almost two."

My triumph was short-lived, naturally. The next night Jules ate nothing but almonds and one carrot. The night after that, nothing at all, and the next one, a banana. Still, progress had been made, and I went about my life with new confidence. Several days later, I got him to eat fish sticks again by giving him a fork, something he'd never been interested in before. As he stabbed his fish with it and said "Press!" I looked out the dining room windows and noticed that the trees in the park across the street were starting to lose their leaves.

I watched the light fail over the thinning leaves and a calm came over me. My son was eating fish. If he had mastered it at home, maybe I could do so at work.

❖ Lobster à l'Américaine à la Steve and Melanie

- 3 1½-pound live lobsters
- 3 tablespoons olive oil
- 1 medium carrot, finely diced
- 1 medium onion, finely diced
- salt and pepper to taste
- 3 tablespoons minced shallots
- 1 clove mashed garlic
- ⅓ cup cognac
- 1 pound whole, peeled canned tomatoes, chopped, without the juice
- 2 tablespoons tomato paste
- 1 cup fish stock
- 1½ cups dry white wine or white vermouth
- 2 tablespoons chopped parsley
- 1 tablespoon chopped tarragon
- 6 tablespoons softened butter
- 2 cups long-grain white rice (basmati will work, too)

1. Have a stiff drink.

2. Open your, or someone's, copy of *MtAoFC* to page 223.

3. Drink some more when you see the length of the recipe.

4. Prep all the vegetables and herbs as above, then take your lobsters out of the refrigerator and observe them silently, preferably with a friend, long enough to arouse the suspicions of anyone in the next room.

5. When those people wander into the kitchen to see what's going on, make one of them kill the lobsters.

6. Put your child to bed and follow the rest of the recipe as written by Julia.

7. Serve the lobster and resulting sauce arranged on a ring of rice, decorated with herbs. Vow that you will never make it again.

Serves 4.

❖ Pasta with Delicata Squash, Sage, and Pine Nuts

2 small or 1 large delicata squash (about 2 pounds)

1 medium red onion

2 tablespoons butter

½ cup pine nuts

½ cup sage leaves, shredded or minced

1 pound spaghetti (though you can use another shape of
    pasta like penne or rigatoni or fusilli)

1. Preheat oven to 350 degrees.
2. Wash the squash well (you'll be eating the skin), split it or them in half lengthwise, and scoop out the seeds.
3. Place the halves face down on a baking sheet and roast in the oven for 20 minutes.
4. While the squash is roasting, mince the red onion and heat a big pot of salted water to a boil for the pasta.
5. In a frying pan, melt the butter over medium heat, then add the onion and turn the heat down to low so that the onion cooks very slowly and caramelizes.
6. Add the pine nuts to the onion and cook, still over low heat, until they're lightly browned. Then add the sage, cook for about a minute, and turn off the heat.
7. Remove the squash from the oven and take it off the pan to cool.
8. By this time the pasta water should be boiling. Add the spaghetti.
9. Turn the heat back on, very low, under the onion/pine nut/sage mixture to warm it up a bit. Cut the cooled squash into rough cubes.
10. Drain the pasta and combine it with the squash and the onion mixture in a big bowl. Serve with grated parmesan cheese.

Serves 2 as main dish with leftovers.

9

❖

Night Shift

"Oh, you'll like Joe Angello," David had said to me with a mysterious smile more than once since I'd started in the kitchen.

If Laura was around, she'd chime in. "Yeah," she'd say, "he's a character."

They both talked about Joe a lot, always very fondly, and always with a chuckle. For some reason, I had formed an idea of him as a jolly, prosperous, perhaps slightly overweight man of about sixty who loved local and organic produce so much he had founded a company to make sure it got to people who wanted it. I pictured him like Oz, behind the curtain, secretly pulling the levers and pushing the buttons that first collected produce and then distributed it to all his customers.

I had no idea, of course, what "distribute it" actually meant. I just knew that somehow boxes of produce, like the ones I had filled at Lucky Dog, made it from the fields to Brooklyn in the white Angello's truck that pulled up outside the restaurant every Thursday. I also knew that without someone like the mythic Joe, the farmers would spend a lot more time selling their product and a lot less time growing it. They'd be at greenmarket tables all the time instead of in their fields, and they'd have no way to expand the market for their food beyond the places where they could drive conveniently. As Richard Giles said to me at one point, "Without Joe, we would be a very different farm. Without the system to efficiently move food, even the short distance from here to New York City, we have no hope of competing with West Coast food. If we're only feeding our own family and the families in our village, then we're living in a very narrow world." Then, further burnishing the legend that had formed in my mind, he added, "And Joe is a rare man."

At last I had to see for myself. Who was this one-man empire with values and character to spare? On a Wednesday morning in October, I took the train up to Hudson, New York (seated, naturally, in front of a woman with a baby of about ten months who was telling someone on her cell phone, "He eats whatever we eat, just cut up into small pieces." I maturely refrained from turning around and making a face at her). An Angello's employee met the train and drove me (in a pale green Prius hybrid) along a series of deserted roads, past a battered white inn with a sign saying "Bar open 4pm. John Deere tractor 4 Sale," to a small white house at the side of Columbia County Route 8 surrounded by greenery and more empty roads. This was the Angello's office. Behind it was a refrigeration building where the produce and other products the firm distributes—organic yogurts, grass-fed meat, sauerkraut, chocolate, to name a few—were stored between their arrival from their various sources and their departure for their destinations. The company's three trucks were out on the road going as far north as Vermont, one hundred and twenty miles away, picking up the fresh food they'd deliver to stores and restaurants the next day.

Every Tuesday, Angello's checks in with the farms it sells for, about fifteen to twenty of them, to get a list of what they'll have available for pickup on Wednesday, then faxes that list to its roughly fifty buyers throughout the Northeast. The clients look at the list and call in their orders, then the farms harvest accordingly, as I had helped to do at Lucky Dog.

When I entered the office, a full-blown lettuce emergency was in progress. One of the farms that was supposed to supply green lettuce that day had reported that they had no Boston lettuce and no green leaf, only red leaf.

Wondering where the boss was, I tried to get out of the way as the guy who had driven me from the train sat down at his desk and began making frantic phone calls.

There was a thumping of boots on the carpeted stairs.

"This lettuce thing is going down fast," said an amused voice. "And the red leaf is looking kind of sketchy."

There he was: Joe Angello, a youthful-looking forty-six, tall and rail thin with a curly red ponytail, dressed in carpenter jeans and a yellow-and-green plaid shirt under a black fleece vest. So much for my vision of a rotund Santa.

Joe, a Californian by birth with a degree in economics from Berkeley, has been involved with organic food for his entire professional life. He founded Angello's out of his house in 2003 after the only existing local organic distributor succumbed to competition from bigger traditional companies that had observed the growing demand for organic products and responded accordingly. Though he had seen it fail firsthand, to Joe, the need for such a company remained uncomplicated. "I simply felt that a distributor who focused on locally produced goods had a place in the market," he told me. Whether they're selling to small stores, supermarket chains, or restaurants, "the big national distributors function much better with national-type brands. I knew that excellent locally produced organic products existed, but that retailers couldn't get many of them from the big distributors."

He's more than willing to admit that at the beginning his approach was a bit naïve. "My business plan came into being about two years after starting my business," he said wryly. "Not recommended, by the way." But, after all, there are legions of stories about successful companies started on nothing but ideals and sleepless nights, of which there were many in those early years at Angello's.

For the first three years, in fact, Joe did everything himself, from picking up food from the farms to packing the trucks to driving all night to deliver the food on time the next morning. He slept on the couch in his office for about three or four hours a night, and he often took his son, who was seven when Joe started the company, in the truck with him. "He played this little horn to keep me from falling asleep," Joe recalled, shaking his head at the memory.

This was the moment when I first began to understand why people thought of Joe as unusual. Only someone with an insane amount of drive and vision, and an insane amount of optimism to match, would do what he did to get his business up and running. But he did it because he thought it needed to be done, and even six years later, with the company on relatively firm footing, there were sacrifices being made daily. "Survival is success on some level in this business," he said. "Year five was profitable, but our labor cost is still well below the market, especially in terms of benefits. My salary is still very low, and we still operate without health insurance or retirement benefits. Profit is the point. Without profit, our mission is meaningless." (Profit, in this case, meant earning enough to pay decent wages and expand the company, rather than getting rich.)

In spite of this dose of reality, Joe hadn't lost sight of either what made his business work or why he started it. As he put it, "It really comes down to the level of commitment of our customers, and the customers of our customers." Joe depends on people like David and Laura, and David and Laura depend on people like me and Noah, who eat at applewood regularly, all of us in agreement with the sentiment that inspired Joe to start Angello's in the first place. "I thought it was nuts buying lettuce from California when it was growing down the street," he told me, settling into his desk chair. "I still think it's nuts."

Like David, Joe recognized that living in the northeastern part of the United States, as opposed to, say, in Southern California, requires making certain compromises regarding both eating and business. Everything sold by Angello's has to be organic at a minimum, and much of it is biodynamic (meaning it comes from a farm that is essentially a closed circle, providing everything it needs to run, like food and fertilizer, from its own land and animals), but not everything is local. Different times of year call for different parameters when it comes to how far food travels. "We have to go outside the area during our off-season because we have overhead that continues year-round, so we're trying to make ends meet during the winter months," Joe told me. The local growing season runs from about June through October and is really the driving force behind the business, with local produce making up about sixty percent of total sales during those months. Joe relies on local items like breads and dairy products all year, but he also distributes things like apples from the Northwest and avocados from Mexico to make up slack in the slow season.

Though Joe agreed that mass distribution of organic products was better than mass distribution of non-organic products, he was also certain that a company like his, which is committed to supporting local communities and sells their products as much as a means to that end as for any other reason, has a place. "We're not here because of any kind of consumer fad," he told me. "Our goal has always been to keep organic agriculture viable in our local and regional area. And to help protect the farmscape, which is something that people value, I believe, in many ways, but they don't really know how to [help] because they're so far removed from the farm." This struck me as the most apt description yet of me standing in that supermarket produce section a year or so before.

Joe decided to take me along to make produce pickups at nearby farms. While waiting by the front door for him to deal with a pumpkin emergency—"Yes, pie pumpkins," I heard him say on the phone; then, in another conversation, "When you talk to Sean, tell him his jack-o'-lanterns are in"—I scanned the posters and bumper stickers pinned up around the door.

"Think locally, act neighborly."

"Be a local hero. Buy locally grown."

And then, somewhat incongruously, "Skate and destroy," which made sense now that I had met Joe, who had the mellow cool of a California skater rather than the stodginess I associated with a northeastern organic food distributor.

Outside, we climbed into a white refrigerated truck, and I wondered if there were other companies like Angello's, founded on "two beat-up old trucks," as Joe put it, and a lot of hard work. "I don't know the other companies that do what we do," he said, putting the key in the ignition, "but I'm quite sure they exist in different regions with varying levels of success. The farmers' job is hard enough. The prices they get are not as good when they sell to Angello's [as they would be selling directly to consumers], but it's a lot easier and we give them the ability to focus more on good agriculture, efficiency, and productivity, rather than marketing and distribution." Just by being part of Angello's, farmers have their products advertised to chefs and retail outlets every week on the order sheet he sends around. Farms that a chef might never have heard of can quickly become regular suppliers because everyone who orders from Joe trusts his judgment.

As we wound our way around from farm to farm on small roads lined with trees whose leaves were every color of tutti-frutti, I couldn't help mentally calculating all the miles between produce pickups. On the one hand, we were driving a lot. On the other, we were using less fuel than if every farmer had driven his or her own product to New York, something Richard had pointed out to me when we were talking about how many heads of lettuce he could drive to New York versus how many a huge truck, traveling more miles but with more lettuce, could carry either across the country or just down the East Coast, as Joe did. "If it costs more in diesel fuel to get a head of my lettuce to Whole Foods than it costs to get a head of Salinas Valley lettuce there, then I shouldn't be supplying them," he'd said.

"Do you worry about that?" I asked Joe. "Food miles and everything?"

"The reality of it is that food is trucked," he replied. "And it's shipped. There's economies of scale, of putting massive numbers of containers on a big ship and running it from Chile to New York. There was a study done measuring the amount of diesel fuel used per unit of apples and it found that the fuel used trucking it from Washington State was a lot more than the fuel used shipping it from Argentina and Chile. So I don't think anything's really all that cut and dried." Of course, I could hardly expect the head of a trucking company, however small, to tell me he thought he shouldn't be doing it, but Joe did have a point. Food is going to be moved regardless of what anyone argues, so isn't the goal to do it as efficiently as possible? It seemed like another case of there being no either/or choice. Buying local produce to support small nearby farms didn't mean there could be *no* fuel costs associated with it, just lower ones.

But there are a lot of other reasons to consider food miles, beyond fuel efficiency. (Several studies have shown that other actions, such as eating less meat, can do more to combat climate change than buying all your food locally.) For one thing, as I learned over and over on my nights at applewood, food that has traveled a shorter distance is fresher and thus more nutritious and better tasting. Also, buying food is about more than just what you put into your body. Purchasing from small nearby producers helps keep the local economy strong—as Richard said, an economy "based on the dirt"—and helps keep it diverse, too. I could do that, and as long as I did, buying things that had been shipped in no manner diminished my support for local farms. As Joe pointed out, if he didn't sell some food from far away during his slow season, he wouldn't have enough money to do what he does during the local produce season.

On a personal level, Joe had worked out a system that incorporated all of these issues. "I don't eat salad in winter," he told me, "unless it's made from grated carrots, apples, beets, celeriac"—ingredients he could get locally. "But some things, like citrus and avocados, just don't grow here, and I don't think it's healthy to totally deprive myself of some of life's wonderful foods and beverages like tropical fruits, coffee, tea, whole cane sugar." Like David ordering his strawberries from California and Richard with his Florida oranges on cold winter mornings, Joe had found the balance, and it seemed like the same one I was reaching myself. As the cold weather came around, I knew, I was going to be eating more beet salads and fewer greens than last winter, this time not out of guilt but understanding.

We drove on, and seeing so many small farms made me want to take Jules along on these visits so that he could see them, too. Otherwise his only knowledge of farms would come from "Old MacDonald" and Richard Scarry books. I suddenly found it peculiar that parents like Noah and me spend so much time reading our kids books like these and emphasizing their importance when many of us have so little experience with their subject matter. "Farm animals and that small farm sort of thing, which is so inherent in us as a culture, I think is dangerously close to being lost," Joe said wistfully. (In fact, the number of small farms in America rose from 2002 to 2007, though most of them, like Cato Corner in the old days, are run by people who have other jobs to support themselves and their crops or animals. Almost half of America's farms make less than twenty-five hundred dollars a year in sales, while five percent of them—the huge ones—account for seventy-five percent of what we eat.)

While buying Joe's products might not be the most direct way or the only way to help save farmland, it at least starts a chain reaction that can lead to change and preservation. "We need to create an economy for local organic agriculture in such a way that the children growing up on these farms want to continue farming," Joe explained. "And that's really what it's about for us. Because if they don't, who's going to do it? Where is that farm going to go?"

It was lunchtime, so we pulled into the parking lot of a diner, the only option nearby. "I think what it boils down to is understanding the cost of paying nothing for our food," Joe finished up. "Not only personally, but socially and culturally. These are the questions I ask. Food is a very important part of who we are as human beings. Why is it that we think it should cost nothing? Something that's that important to us?" Of course, as Richard had told me, it doesn't cost nothing at all. We simply perceive that it does since it's much easier to focus on that extra dollar at the farm market or the price difference between organic and conventional milk than it is to grasp concepts like farm subsidies, the connection between rising health care costs and the food we eat, and other hidden expenses. Even families who can barely afford to buy food are paying in one way or another. As Pollan wrote in *The Omnivore's Dilemma*, "Cheap industrial food is heavily subsidized in many ways such that its price in the supermarket does not reflect its real cost. But until the rules that govern our food system change, organic or sustainable food is going to cost more at the register, more than some people can afford. Yet for the majority of us the story is not quite so simple. As a society, we Americans spend only a fraction of our disposable income feeding ourselves—about a tenth, down from a fifth in the 1950s. This suggests that there are many of us who could afford to spend more if we chose to. After all, it isn't only the elite who in recent years have found an extra fifty or one hundred dollars each month to spend on cell phones or televisions."

Inside the diner, which was decorated with innumerable plastic figurines and plants, I ate a grilled cheese sandwich that tasted more like plastic than anything else. Joe, after considering the menu at length, ordered fish and chips. The whole lunch cost fifteen dollars, far less than the organic apples and potatoes I had recently bought at the farmers' market.

"This is like the anti-Angello's lunch," I told Joe, wiping the grease off my hands with a paper napkin. "I kind of can't believe you're eating it."

Joe grinned. "Life is full of paradoxes," he said.

It was late afternoon when we got back to the Angello's office, and two trucks of produce were being unpacked onto the loading dock of the refrigeration building. The third truck had gotten stuck in the mud at one of the Vermont farms and, after a long delay while the driver waited for a tow truck, was finally on its way back.

Hanging on the office wall was a hand-drawn diagram of the three trucks that were going out to deliver that night. Each one had a picture of which orders went on which pallet, and where in each truck the pallets went, so that the right pallet would be accessible at each drop-off location. It was a highly efficient, if distinctly old-fashioned, system. Which, it turns out, is what you need when you're dealing with small farmers and the amazing variety of produce they grow. Nothing can be overly computerized or outsourced; there has to be someone at each stage—farmer, packer, destination—who knows what each product looks like and where it comes from. A company like Angello's can handle the variations, and similarly small companies can sell them. At chain stores, by contrast, even those interested in selling local produce, according to Joe, "there are real challenges to local growing, just because of the variety and the labeling. Labeling's a big issue in those stores because everything's computerized."

Big stores are set up to receive large amounts of the same produce over and over again because they buy from large farms which grow enough to supply all their outlets. Small farms, as I'd seen during the lettuce emergency at Angello's when I first arrived, aren't always so consistent. The farmers try new things each year, and sometimes disaster strikes, as it did during the 2009 tomato blight. But even without disasters, the way small farms work doesn't fit very well with corporate structures. At a place like Lucky Dog, for example, sometimes the kale is green, sometimes it's Lacinato, sometimes it's rainbow, and sometimes what was ordered isn't what shows up. This is fine at a place like applewood, where dinner can be made out of whatever arrived, or at a local grocery store where the owner can just write a new sign by hand, but it creates what amounts to a culture clash at bigger firms. "Everything's computerized," Joe continued, "and the cashiers don't really know an apple from an orange. I mean, they do, but all they know is that it's got a [scannable] PLU number which has a code." I had already seen the incredible amount of work it took just to get the produce grown, picked, and delivered to the Angello's warehouse with some kind of label on it. "Now imagine you have to do different labels for different kinds of kale," Joe went on. "And the bar code tag. And then every tomato has to have stickers with the tomato PLU, and I'm also trying to promote the farm with labels. So . . ." His voice trailed off as the packing staff assembled on the dock.

The crew members who loaded and unloaded the produce were all in their teens or early twenties. I met Randy, the warehouse manager, working a shift from ten A.M. to midnight; Heather, his fiancée, who was studying fashion in Manhattan and worked from eight-fifteen P.M. to midnight; Jim, Randy's brother, working from noon to midnight; and Steve, working from four to eleven. They had all been hired by word of mouth or an ad in the local paper.

At six-thirty, pizza arrived in the office and we all went over there to grab slices to take back to the loading dock.

"It's nice organic pizza!" Joe said with a sly look.

"But it's local!" said the accountant, who had just stopped in to run some numbers.

Back in the refrigeration building, before we even finished chewing, Randy yanked on a long rope that hung from the ceiling. A huge door in the wall slid open, revealing the cooler room. We put on our jackets and headed in, and Randy pulled another rope to make the door slide shut behind us.

　　We were sealed into a vast, windowless concrete bunker, seven thousand square feet with a twenty-foot-high ceiling, filled with produce and dry goods stacked almost to the ceiling on wooden pallets or wooden shelving. It was cold, about thirty-nine degrees (fortunately I had several extra long-sleeved shirts in my bag, which was stowed in a camper parked in another one of the warren of unused concrete rooms that made up the building). I shivered a bit as I took in the contents of the room. There was a small desk in the middle for keeping the orders straight, and the rest of the space was filled with more food than I had ever seen in one place in my life. There were boxes of sauerkraut, yogurt, milk, grass-fed beef, chocolate bars, and numerous other items, but the produce was what interested me most. There was arugula and bok choy and three kinds of chard, at least a dozen varieties of apple, pears, cabbage, and not just white cauliflower but purple and orange, too. There were jewel yams and garnet yams and about ten different squashes, including one called Thelma Sanders, which seemed more like the name of a third-grade teacher than a squash to me. There were fingerling potatoes and blue potatoes and white potatoes. There were leeks and there were peppers, several dozen kinds, from serrano to cherry bomb to green bell. Next to them were seven varieties of eggplant and five kinds of radishes. There were plums and melons and turnips and rutabaga, and all of it had come from no farther away than Vermont. Surrounded by this abundance, I found it hard to believe that in a few months nothing would be growing in this part of the country but cabbage, potatoes, a few kinds of squash, and the occasional apple, turnip, or carrot.

Heavy lifting seemed like the only way to warm up, so when Heather grabbed a pallet list, I followed her. We took an empty wooden pallet off a pile and put it on the floor, then started circling the room collecting the items in the first order. Boxes of preserves and other jarred items went on the bottom, then bags of apples and parsnips, a few boxes of squash, a bag of beets. On top went lighter boxes of kale, spinach, and dandelion greens. Then we started another order on the other half of the same pallet. When it was done, we moved on to the next order, wandering the aisles of bright orange squash and purple potatoes and neon-green apples with lists in our hands, calling for help when the boxes were too big for us to pick up on our own.

As we were loading pallets and I was running in and out of the cooler room to add more shirts to my layers, Ambrosio, the driver whose truck had been stuck in the mud, appeared. After he unloaded his produce, Joe told him I would be accompanying him on the Brooklyn route that night. Then Ambrosio went home to sleep. "Regreso a las dos y media," he told me with a wave. Two-thirty? He'd pick me (and the pallets) up and we'd leave at two-thirty A.M.? I went back to my packing to avoid dwelling on this shocking news.

Too many fifty-pound boxes of Adirondack Blue potatoes and twenty-five-pound bags of parsnips later, around eleven P.M., I said goodnight and went to the deserted camper to try to get a few hours of sleep before my date with Ambrosio. I felt I had barely closed my eyes (and maybe I hadn't—there are many less creepy places to sleep than an isolated camper in a mostly empty concrete-walled processing plant in the middle of nowhere) when my watch alarm went off just before two-thirty. Adding a hat to my collection of five shirts, fleece vest, and sweater, I staggered out to the loading dock, where Ambrosio—the same driver, I suddenly realized, who had come into the potato field at Lucky Dog to help us dig—was loading the last pallet onto the truck. He smiled and said, "Vamos?"

It was pitch black outside and pouring rain as we pulled away. "Te gustas la música Mejicana?" Ambrosio asked, punching at the radio.

"Sí," I replied, as the wipers swiped and the salsa music blasted. I noticed he had a Coke in the drink holder and wondered again why I was so often caught without either coffee or enough clothing.

An hour later we made a stop, still in utter darkness, at a gas station for Krispy Kreme donuts (again, not organic, but probably local, at least in terms of where they'd been baked) and a Coke, neither of which was enough to keep me from dozing.

We made it to Brooklyn at five-fifteen A.M. At our first two stops, small groceries, the stores weren't open so we snoozed in the truck each time until they were, then Ambrosio spent about forty minutes unloading at each one.

At our third stop, a small gourmet market filled with young families and hipsters buying coffee on their way to work, I had the odd sensation of viewing my own life from the outside, as if it were a movie. Normally I would have been one of those people dawdling over pastry with a stroller or grabbing a cup of coffee on the way to the subway. Now I was in the truck, wondering if they even noticed we were there. I had never paid the slightest attention to any of the delivery trucks in my neighborhood. The fact that Joe's trucks brought food no one else cared to distribute made me wonder about the stories behind all the other trucks out on the street, dropping off crates and boxes.

But even if those work-bound urbanites didn't know we were there, someone else did. Ambrosio finished unloading, and before he went in to settle the bill he handed me his cell phone through the truck window.

It was Joe.

"You're a trouper!" he said upon learning I was still along for the ride. (Though, really, where else could I have been?)

Recalling that Joe had done this every week for years—pickup, pack, drive, collapse—made me determined to survive the rest of the stops in good humor. We went to a food co-op I didn't recognize, then to the butcher four blocks from my apartment where I often shopped without ever considering where their products came from, then to a market two blocks from my apartment, and finally to the main drag in my neighborhood.

I was almost home free. After just one more stop, at applewood, I would be able to stagger home to bed. It was nine-thirty in the morning and I couldn't believe how alert Ambrosio seemed after sleeping five hours, driving two and a half, and lugging heavy boxes all over Brooklyn. Unlike him, I wasn't lifting anything or even moving from my seat in the truck cab, and all I wanted to do was to quietly pass out somewhere.

Naturally, there was no parking. We circled the block several times, Ambrosio muttering under his breath in Spanish. I was getting desperate. Then, as we turned down the street to the avenue one last time, a beacon appeared.

It was Frank, whom I had come to think of as applewood's "fixer." Short and stocky, with a crew cut and a sweet face, Frank had worked in two other, much lower-scale restaurants before landing at applewood. He had biked up to the door the summer before it opened, while David and his father were building the kitchen, and been hired on the spot. He had two young sons named Joshua and Brian (Joshua and Jules were about the same age), and it was obvious to me that he was one of the magicians behind the scenes who made applewood run so smoothly.

Frank's official duties included tasks like laundry and inventory, but if you had any kind of emergency — beets needed to be peeled in record time, you had spilled vast quantities of oil on the floor, you couldn't find the chives, or anything else — Frank was your man. He knew where everything was and how to extract it from its hiding place in seconds. He was also a crack gnocchi maker and in charge of butchering all the fish, both skills he had learned at applewood.

That morning, apparently, he was also in charge of valet parking. He had seen us circling the block and now, dressed in his chef's jacket and pants, waved us into a parking space he had saved for us by stepping into it when he saw some-one pull out.

"Hi, Melanie!" he said cheerfully as I hurled myself from the truck, as though he was used to seeing me arrive with the produce every Thursday morning.

"Hi," I managed to say. "I'm going home."

"Sleep well," he said with a beatific smile.

"You, too," I mumbled, turning up the block as he shook his head and went through the restaurant's green doors and back to the kitchen.

10

❖

Rich in Imperfections

As WINTER NEARED, the produce turning up at the restaurant began to range in color from brown to yellow to beige. There was an occasional dash of red or purple from beets or red cabbage or a red wine reduction in a sauce, but mostly we were in the land of root vegetables. It was getting so cold outside that it actually felt good to enter the kitchen in mid-afternoon (though by the middle of dinner service I was still drenched with sweat, which froze to the back of my neck on the way home). I went back to prep in the afternoon and garde manger during service, which by this time felt profoundly familiar and comfortable. I could knock out a beet salad like nobody's business, and I'd even learned to mince chives into the required paper-thin bits.

Then one chilly afternoon I arrived to find something unexpected at garde manger. A box of lettuce. Lettuce in winter.

"Where is *this* from?" I asked David.

"I just *had* this conversation with one of our regulars," David sighed, looking slightly aggrieved.

The lettuce was from Florida, and apparently someone had pitched a small fit at dinner a few nights earlier about the fact that it was not local.

"So what did you tell him?" I asked. By this point I had my own ideas about why it might make sense to buy lettuce from a small farm a little farther away than Lucky Dog, but I was curious to hear David's take.

As if reading my mind, David said, "It's local-*ish*,"—he meant East Coast instead of West Coast, so at least closer to home if not all that close—"and it's biodynamic." Then he reminded me of the difference between buying as a single shopper and buying as a restaurant owner. "The business outweighs it. People won't come if all you serve is rutabaga. Nothing grows in the Hudson River valley at this time of year. Nothing. You'd have garlic."

"True," I said. "And I guess you wouldn't eat just garlic at home. You have to tempt your family sometimes the way you tempt your customers." (I felt qualified to say this as by this time I was a master at efforts to tempt a certain person to eat.)

"Yeah," David agreed. "I bought the kids those little grape cherry tomatoes yesterday because it works. You put it in their lunch and they eat it." This was sounding oddly familiar. "We're buying Mexican avocados from Angello's," he went on, "because they vouch for the farmer and said these are good people who are making a commitment and will you please buy some. But then, I'm a sucker." (David often referred to applewood as the "sucker account"; basically, he would buy anything anyone he trusted needed to get rid of, animal, vegetable, or other, figuring they needed to sell it and he could think of something interesting to do with it.)

"We're as local as possible," he continued, "and the important thing is that you think about it." He was at the stove, braising red cabbage in red wine. "But you can't think about it all the time. It's the same thing as with Jules. You know it's a huge pain in the ass to think about every meal, so you can't do it all the time. Sometimes you have to say, 'You know what? I'm going to have the gyro platter from the dirty diner and I'm going to enjoy it.' But you still have the thought process."

(This little speech may have been partly inspired by that day's family meal, deliciously crispy chicken wings with buffalo sauce, which David had picked up frozen at the restaurant supply store where he was buying necessities like sponges and trash bags, then thrown into the deep fryer to everyone's delight.)

Even people who patronize a restaurant like applewood, apparently, sometimes have trouble with the concept of seasonal produce. For every diner arguing about the food miles involved in transporting lettuce from Florida, there was someone who liked the idea of local and seasonal but didn't quite get it. The previous April, a month that everyone in the Northeast pretends is warmer than it actually is just because we're all so sick of our winter coats, someone had written on a comment card: "Loved the meal—but I would like more opportunities for green vegetables as a side." In May, when some greens were available, what Laura referred to as "the nightly salad fight" began with diners who didn't think what the restaurant was calling a salad—often pea shoots or some other early spring green—qualified. "If the farmers don't have it, we don't have it," Laura would say (the Florida lettuce being a rare exception made, again, because Joe had vouched for the farmer).

Like David, I was far less draconian in my produce choices at home because I had no alternative if Jules was going to eat anything fresh. California was plenty close enough for me. Noah and I had figured out by this point that Jules's tastes leaned toward the crunchy. This had led to the realization that he wouldn't try pasta because it jiggled on the plate. We accepted this, but began biting into various foods demonstratively to indicate their crispness in order to get him to try them. Since it was winter and he would only eat raw vegetables that crunched noisily, we bought him organic carrots and red peppers grown thousands of miles away and turned a blind eye to the local issue. I knew David understood, and I was pretty sure Richard and Joe would understand, too.

Not long before the Florida lettuce appeared, when there was still a little bit of colorful produce on the menu, David had asked me if I wanted to go back to the fish station—with him on backup, of course. About two hours into my first shift after this conversation, when the skills from my first stint on fish were coming back to me and everything was going along just fine, the New York City Department of Health sent someone out for a surprise inspection. Clipboard in hand, the official appeared in the kitchen—a dark presence in his navy blue cap and official city-issued windbreaker among all the white-jacketed chefs—at around seven-thirty, just as the dinner rush was starting and just as I was putting my third order of scallops into the pan.

While two servers ran downstairs to cover the whole animals in the walk-in—each carcass was required to be forty degrees inside, which they were, but David was worried about getting an inspector who had never seen one before and might decide that even though they were completely legal and being stored properly, they were unappealing and thus a violation—everyone in the kitchen tried to behave as though nothing unusual was going on. We pitched our quart containers of water (no drinks allowed in the kitchen, for some reason none of us understood). We checked the temperature in our lowboys (they, too, had to be forty degrees). The man with the clipboard was making notes, and I imagined his report as I hovered over my scallops: "Restaurant employing fake chef."

I counted it as a mark of my growing competence that in spite of the various distractions, when I next looked down at my pan the scallops were perfectly done and ready to plate.

The scallops, in fact, were the least of my problems; now the canister of clean spoons in water that usually sat on the counter had disappeared. (Was there some kind of ordinance against this, too, or had someone just panicked and made a clean sweep?) My fish spatula was now in the sink to the left of the stove, where the stick blender was usually kept, in another canister with water running on it constantly. Every time I needed the spatula I instinctively reached to the counter, then wasted time turning around and fishing it out of the sink. I was whipping around so much I felt slightly dizzy. No one else had what they needed at hand, either; the kitchen slowed to a crawl.

"Go out there and tell your tables what's going on," David said to the servers, who were getting antsy waiting for their plates. "Buy them a drink if you have to."

It was unusually quiet in the kitchen. Only the swishing of the dishwasher and the infrequent clattering of plates in the busing tub—if very little is going out, very little comes back in—broke the tense hush.

The mood was grim. The dining room was full.

And I cooked. I just kept working, and David, busy running up and down the stairs to be sure everything was okay in the basement and trying to chat up the inspector, left me on my own.

I made two red radish–jalapeño salads with grilled melon. I made two foie gras appetizers with grape reduction, basil oil, and grilled walnut bread. "Chef, can you grill this?" I asked Sarah over and over, handing her melon or walnut bread. And when she handed them back the third or fourth time with "Here you go, Chef," I was not too stressed to miss the moniker—I was in!—even though she was probably just too distracted to realize she was using it. I made two celery soups and a lobster broth; four orders of trout with spiced chickpeas, Italian peppers, and apple-cilantro relish; five orders of scallops with grilled red onions, tomatillo salsa, and sweet corn soup; nine orders of halibut with rapini and chanterelle mushroom ragout and a mushroom-onion purée; and three groupers (all of which I remembered to remove from the oven in time) with collard greens and sautéed green onions. Somewhere I found the time to dip the cut sides of a dozen tomatillo halves into buttermilk and then cornmeal and fry them, cornmeal side down, for an appetizer being put together at garde manger.

It was by no means a perfect performance. I burned myself five times, as I learned later by counting the angry red hash marks on my forearms. I also dropped a pot of rapini with chanterelles on the floor, where it splashed up onto my legs. David, passing by at that exact moment, said, "Are you okay?"

"Yes! Yes!" I barked, brushing him aside. Who had time to talk? I was a chef!

Slowly the bottleneck eased, the man with the clipboard moved to the bar to write more notes and be ogled by the diners (David heard the following week that the restaurant had passed the inspection without a hitch), and when I next looked at the clock, it was eleven-thirty. The shift was over. Sarah and I, as was the custom for whoever was on the line, cooked pieces of fish and meat and served them, with whatever sides we had left over from dinner, to the dishwashers, who would be cleaning the kitchen long after we left.

After scrubbing down my station with soap and bleach, I drifted the two blocks to my apartment in a daze, too wiped out to bask in the glow of my first solo performance. I took a hot shower to wash off the stink of sweat and fish, then got into bed next to Noah and waited for the adrenaline to wear off, which took until around two A.M.

Somewhere in my insomniac musings, I thought about the calculated risk David had taken by leaving me alone at the stove, and then about the many compromises and risks he and Laura had made and taken to open applewood, like working late into the night for months with two small children asleep in the back room, children they then had to cart home—and get up with the next morning. (I had cut a deal with Noah so that he got up with Jules on the mornings after my restaurant shifts since he went to bed earlier than I did, but no one was getting to bed early in the Shea household.)

Working at applewood, I gradually discovered that the charmed vision the restaurant's customers had all had of Laura, David, and their children in applewood's early days was, like so many charmed visions, partly false. When the restaurant opened, Laura was just a few weeks away from giving birth to Tatum. She was enormous, and it seemed to Noah and me when we ate there that first week that starting a restaurant was terrifying and odds-defying enough without being eight and a half months pregnant on top of it.

And then, the next time we ate there, Laura was no longer pregnant and instead had tied to her hip in a sling a plump, rosy, blond baby girl. By the time Tatum was a month old, she could frequently be found at the table near the fireplace wearing nothing but a cloth diaper, keeping warm with a group of delighted customers while Laura dashed off to take care of some task. Diners often requested a viewing, and when something went awry at a table, whether it was a service error or a long wait for the food, a surprise visit from Tatum could smooth over almost anything, almost instantly.

Customers (and restaurant critics, who couldn't help penning what Laura referred to affectionately as "reviews of Tatum") adored Tatum, who seemed, quite literally, a bright shiny emblem of all that eating well could produce. From the diners' point of view (including mine), the scene was positively bucolic. Meanwhile, behind the scenes, her parents were close to losing their minds.

"The thing that was pushing me to the brink was having to take the girls home at the end of the night every night," Laura told me. "It was so hard to have worked this really long day and then have to wheel the buggy in, push all the tables aside, get it set up with blankets, have the staff be quiet, lower the lights, run the girls through the greasy kitchen, get them wrapped up, back the buggy out, go home, and then once we got home open it up, unwrap them, run them up two flights of stairs. That was the worst. I couldn't keep doing it every night. They just keep getting heavier!"

For the first three years of Sophie's life, back when the Sheas were living in Chicago, Laura had rarely left her child's side. After Tatum's arrival, she was surprised to find herself wishing she had someone to care for the children at home while she worked. "In Chicago, I would get so sad when I'd see kids at the park with their nannies," she said, laughing at her former self. "How sad that people choose to let their children be raised by nannies, and if everyone was just a great parent like me the world would be a much better place." Her voice took on a mock-snooty tone. "'At least

I'm here to set an example and my child is perfect and your child is whining because you work!'"

After the Sheas made the move to New York, Laura still refused to budge on her decision to stay home with her child. "David had a really hard time finding work and I still wasn't working," she remembered. "I was just being Sophie's mom. Self-righteous Sophie's mom." Eventually, after David's burger-joint job and their decision to open applewood, she changed her mind, and it was the start of a new life for them all.

"We wanted to put in the work and the effort for ourselves, not punch the clock for somebody else," David told me. "How that was going to materialize or what form it was going to take was the question. In the debate or discussion trying to figure out what *it* was going to be, how it would work with having kids was a big part. One scenario we came up with in the middle of the night was, 'We'll never see the kids, the kids will hate the restaurant, we're going to have to force them to be there when they don't want to be, they're never going to get to do kid stuff, we're going to be stuck with this restaurant, stuck with kids that hate the restaurant.' And then obviously that didn't happen."

I came to believe that the Sheas had survived those exhausting early years at applewood because they had decided to simply love the restaurant, the kids, the whole messy, impossible package, and to worry about the details as they cropped up. Even Tatum's birth was that kind of detail. When Laura went into labor one night around midnight, just after a dinner shift, her first thought was, "The minute I say something, they're going to make me go home, and I have stuff to do that nobody else, including David, knows how to do." Though she had planned to take a few weeks off, she ended up having Tatum early the next morning, a Friday, and going back to work on Saturday. "I remember watching her waddle down the street with Tatum in the sling on Saturday morning," David said, "and I knew it was fine." He added with a laugh, "And it ruined any hope of me ever complaining about anything again."

Laura explained, "I took exactly the opposite attitude I had with Sophie. Get out there and do something! With Sophie I was all about nursing and slings and attachment parenting and I really believed in it. It's not that I stopped believing in those ideals, it's just that I don't think they have to be mutually exclusive. It was a learning process for me, becoming the person and mother I ended up being."

Part of the reason the Sheas were able to pull off what they did—opening and running their own restaurant while raising two small children—was their staff, all of whom seemed to accept as a matter of course that there would be children around, especially Tatum when she was too young to have a bedtime in the back room like Sophie. From the dining room during dinner service, it was not uncommon to look through the glass-paned door into the kitchen and glimpse one of the servers or dishwashers carrying her around while Laura was otherwise occupied, as though it was the most natural thing in the world to have a newborn in a kitchen where open flames were going all the time and where the temperature often topped a hundred degrees.

Family of all kinds was everywhere at applewood. One day when I was watching Frank take apart an enormous tilefish, dark gray with bright yellow spots, I asked him where he'd learned how to do it. He said he'd done some bass at his previous jobs, then gestured toward David, put down his knife, raised his hands to his heart and said, "He's my teacher," in a tone of voice I hope to inspire in someone someday. Frank's younger brother, Joseph, was the assistant dishwasher. He had started at the restaurant just days after I began working in the kitchen, and six months later he was learning how to do garde manger.

Another crucial staff member was Pete, whose brother Johnny was the main dishwasher. Pete was in his late thirties, muscled and bald with a little mustache, and like Frank he had been at applewood since it opened. He had several ex-wives and a smattering of children in various places, and once said to me mournfully, "I think with this"—gesturing to his heart—"instead of this"—pointing to his head.

Together, these people kept the restaurant running. As David mused, "When this place closes, it'll probably only be me, Laura, Frank, and Pete left standing." Pete worked the floor, delivering the bread and daily spreads that were served to every table after ordering, clearing plates, and running food from the kitchen. When things were slow, he was generally on hand to make coffee with a thick layer of sugar at the bottom for the kitchen staff—on some nights, the only thing that got me through—and to challenge us to feats of strength like trying to lift our own body weight on one arm by placing a hand flat on the stainless steel counter and pushing up (even in a kitchen like applewood's, you sometimes run out of things to pickle and cure in your downtime).

Frank, in addition to his kitchen skills, had an enviable inborn talent: he was an organizational genius. Every Thursday he would tackle the challenge of fitting an insane amount of produce, fish, and dairy into a walk-in that wasn't nearly big enough for it, while leaving room for the three or four whole animals that would be delivered later in the day and had to be hung in there until they could be butchered. Every Thursday I wondered how he could possibly do it, and every Thursday, within a few hours, he did it. He even managed to make the chaos in the walk-in functional; there always seemed to be a whole pig positioned perfectly as a handhold when you needed to balance on a box of wine bottles to reach something on a high shelf. After watching this for a few months, I mentioned to David that Frank could probably get rich quick if he opened a side business organizing people's closets, and that I would happily be his first customer. David laughed, but I could see that he didn't find the thought of losing Frank to his inner Martha Stewart entirely funny.

"Frank is greatly determined and a tough guy," he said with affection. "One in a million." Then he went off to consult with him about what supplies needed to be ordered that week.

The Monday before Thanksgiving, I went to applewood to help with the catering for people who had ordered free-range turkeys from Vermont and sides to go with them.

(David drew the line at actually cooking the turkeys, though no doubt he would have had plenty of takers for that service, too.) In a single afternoon, when the restaurant was closed, Greg, Sarah, David, and I made sweet potato purée for fifty-two; herbed new potatoes for thirty-two; a mix of roasted carrots, rutabaga, parsnips, and potatoes for ninety-six; butternut squash soup for ninety-two; cranberry chutney for eighty-four; pecan stuffing for ninety-six; and turkey gravy for eighty-four. Some of the portion numbers, typed up on a sheet that had been stuck into the ticket rail at garde manger, were imprecise, but it was not a time of year for stiffing anyone. "Basically, every quart container should serve about three people," David had written at the bottom of the portion list. "Overestimate. Give more when in doubt and all will be well."

The catering work got me in the mood for cooking our own Thanksgiving dinner, which would include a Vermont turkey given to us by David and Laura as thanks for my help with the catering. On Thanksgiving Day, as Noah and I prepared dinner for my family and part of his, Jules played at our feet in the kitchen, making us pretend coffee and eagerly waiting for his cousins to arrive. We made the Brussels sprouts from a doctored recipe a dear friend had clipped from the *New York Times* years ago. (It contains my favorite penciled-in note ever: "I usually add a stick of butter here.") We cooked the sweet potatoes with maple syrup and chipotle peppers, to remind Noah of where he came from. And even though by this time I knew many ways to prepare stuffing, I made it with chestnuts, exactly the way my mother, who would be with us that day, had made it since she met my father. We brined and cooked the turkey as David had suggested ("More salt than you would ever think") because he was a chef, but also because, by now, he was our friend.

When we sat down to the meal, my mind traveled two blocks down the street to applewood, where the Sheas and everyone on the restaurant staff who wasn't going somewhere else were celebrating. I was facing our dining room windows, and out in the park the tree branches were completely bare and stark black against the fading light, glittering with raindrops from a cold afternoon shower. As I looked around the table at our families—at my nephews who ate anything, at Noah's nieces who were old enough that no one minded what they ate anymore, at Jules who was stuffing himself with bread (hallelujah!) and nothing else—I thought of James Merrill's wonderful lines about loving people in spite of their flaws (or their eating habits). In the final section of his poem "Variations: The Air Is Sweetest That a Thistle Guards" (1951), Merrill wrote:

> . . . not love, great pearl
> That swells around a small unlovely need;
> Nor love whose fingers tie the bows of birth
> Upon the sorry present. Love merely as the best
> There is, and one would make the best of that
> By saying how it grows and in what climates,
> By trying to tell the crystals from the branch,
> Stretching that wand then toward the sparkling wave.

To say at the end, however we find it, good,
Bad, or indifferent, it helps us, and the air
Is sweetest there. The air is very sweet.

I passed the bread basket to Jules and the potatoes to my
mother. Give more when in doubt and all will be well.

❖ Brined Turkey

7 quarts water, plus more if needed
1½ cups salt (though this is imprecise)
about 2 tablespoons juniper berries
about 2 tablespoons whole black peppercorns
3 bay leaves
maybe 3 or 4 onions, coarsely chopped
ditto on the carrots, also coarsely chopped
any other herb or flavoring that sounds good (thyme,
    rosemary, garlic, etc.)
1 18–20-pound turkey

1. In a large pot, bring 1 quart of the water, along with
the salt, juniper berries, peppercorns, bay leaves, onions, carrots, and whatever else you decide to add, to a boil. Then
turn off the heat.

2. While the above mixture is cooling, place the turkey in
a large plastic bag (a garbage bag will do, though actual brin-
ing bags are now available).

3. Pour the remaining 6 quarts of water into the bag. They should almost cover the turkey.

4. Now add the spice and water mixture from the pot. If the turkey is not completely covered, add more water until it is.

5. Close the bag tightly and leave the turkey to brine for about 24 hours. You can leave it out—no need to clear off that shelf in the fridge that you really need for all the side dish ingredients. We do and haven't killed anyone yet.

6. The next day, remove the turkey, dry it, and roast as usual.

Serves 10.

❖ Jean's Brussels Sprouts

(adapted first by Jean and then by me from the *New York Times Magazine*)

---

5 pints Brussels sprouts
½ pound bacon, diced
½ cup pine nuts
3 shallots (instead of scallions, as per Jean), minced fine
1 stick butter
freshly ground black pepper

1. Cut off tough stalk and outer leaves of sprouts. Place them in a food processor to shred coarsely. [Or, if you're like me, just chop them up with a big knife because you

never bought a food processor. They end up shredded either way.]

2. Fry the bacon in a large skillet until it is crisp. Remove and drain on paper towels. Add the shallots and pine nuts to the fat remaining in the pan and stir over medium heat until lightly browned, about 2–3 minutes.

3. Add the shredded sprouts. Cook, stirring, over medium heat until they are cooked through but still crisp. Here Jean says, "I add about a stick of butter while they cook, stirring it in approximately a tablespoon at a time, since the bacon fat isn't nearly enough to keep the shredded sprouts [5 pints, after all] from getting dry."

4. Then she says, having gleefully abandoned the recipe altogether by this point, "Keep stirring and shoveling the sprouts around so the bottom layer doesn't burn. It takes longer than six to eight minutes [what the recipe says]—more like ten to fifteen—to cook through."

5. Crumble in the bacon, add the pepper to taste, stir, and serve.

Serves however many people are willing to eat Brussels sprouts—probably about 8, but you may have leftovers.

11

❖

Away in a Manger

At some point, along with the reasonable beliefs that children need to sleep and breathe, the idea that "little children love to dip things" seems to have become a fundamental plank of parenting. In the months when Jules ate the least, people were constantly telling me that they had gotten their little Janie or Jack to eat something by offering a sauce for dunking. Why I bought into this concept given my own sorry history with sauce as a child, I do not know. Nevertheless, we started putting ketchup, the most-mentioned dipping sauce, on Jules's plate with some regularity. Apparently there were parents nationwide whose kids would eat almost anything as long as they could dip it in ketchup first.

For us, unsurprisingly, ketchup did not have the desired effect. Jules would say "Dip dip!" over and over while miming dipping a piece of food into his ketchup without ever actually touching the ketchup, then put the food down, unbitten or even licked. Meanwhile, ketchup itself became his favorite meal. He asked for it constantly and ate it straight with a spoon or a fork. When it was gone, he ignored our pleas to move on to the next food on the plate and excused himself from the table with a polite "Down, peese?" (He had learned how to undo the buckles on his booster seat months before.) Had there been a redeeming aspect to this development—had he, say, branched out to foods with tomato sauce on them, like pizza or pasta—we might have accepted his ketchup craze more graciously.

But there was not. Jules was about to turn two and hadn't expanded his palate in months, with the critical exception of bagels with cream cheese (a true blessing since in New York City you can get one anywhere) plus crackers, bread, and cookies of any kind (meet Young Mr. Carbohydrate, son of Miss Carbohydrate). He had had a three-day love affair with shredded salami—the first meat that had entered his system since the baby food days—but then wouldn't touch it, or any other meat, again. Instead, there were dinners of ketchup and milk and maybe a few carrots, followed by yogurt at bedtime to keep him from waking up hungry at five A.M.

It was December, and it was time for me to flee again, this time to a farm near Andover, Vermont. In my three days there, none of this would be my problem. If someone woke me up in the wee hours crying for food, it would be a cow. Or a goat. Or a lamb. I was going to the source of what we referred to at the restaurant as "the animals."

Every Thursday, sometime between noon and the dinner rush—occasionally *during* the dinner rush—an unmarked white van arrived from a company called Fancy Meats from

Vermont, a cooperative of small farmers, each of whom had joined for the benefit of having their meat distributed in much the same way that Angello's distributed its products. There were fewer farms than Joe had, and they were closer together than his, but the principle was identical: less driving and less marketing by farmers, who could then spend the time tending to their animals and land. The first day I watched the delivery, standing at garde manger shelling peas, I was only dimly aware of the black-garbage-bagged forms being carried in through the dining room over someone's shoulder, some of them with cloven hooves or a head hanging out one end of the bag. Then David sent me down to the walk-in to get a few packages of bacon, and I opened the door to discover two pigs, a goat, two lambs, and a huge hind of veal.

The animals were hanging haphazardly from the shelving in the walk-in, and I, who had never seen a whole dead animal in my life, had to throw not just my shoulder but my entire self against a cold, rubbery-fleshed pig that weighed more than I did, in order to reach the shelf behind it and grab the bacon.

To my surprise, I had felt no revulsion at the sight of the blood-streaked animals hanging by their heels in that claustrophobic space, brushing up against the bright produce; they belonged there, after all. I got my bacon, let the pig swing back into place as I straightened up, and went upstairs to cut lardons for a warm vinaigrette.

And now I was on my way to the place where many of these animals had lived before they ended up on the plates of appreciative applewood diners. I drove about two hundred and fifty miles north, up through Connecticut and Massachusetts, and finally turned onto a narrow winding road lined with bare trees that glittered in the winter afternoon sun. I followed it for a few miles uphill to a clearing at the top of a ridge, where I parked in front of a low white nineteenth-century farmhouse built close to the road with a wooden sign that read "Lovejoy Brook." A small, slightly ramshackle wooden building near the house was connected via a wooden-fenced cow pen to a cedar-shingled round barn a bit higher up on the slope.

The first big snowstorm of the season was predicted for later that weekend, and I could smell it in the air. The frozen ground crunched beneath my feet as I walked to the house and entered a big kitchen with rough-hewn ceiling beams and walls lined with yellow beadboard to waist level with copper pots hanging above it.

There were three stoves: close to the door, a pot-bellied woodburning model with two kettles on it; across the room, a cast-iron behemoth with two ovens; and next to that a regular white metal stove, the only one with burners. A black soapstone sink was framed by dark wood cabinets, and a small iron chandelier hung over a table covered with a red-and-white-checked cloth and holding a pitcher of slightly wilted white roses. Opposite the sink, an incongruously ornate gilt-framed mirror hung between two floor-to-ceiling bookcases of dark wood. Among the titles on the shelves were *The New York Times Cook Book,* something called *Plain Cooking,* several books by Buckminster Fuller, and *A Veterinary Guide for Animal Owners.*

Sitting at the table was Lucy Georgeff, one of the farm-hands, who looked to be in her mid-twenties and had her brown hair in braids. Leaning against the sink was Lydia Ratcliff, the farm's owner, in her early seventies with long, straight white hair, wearing a royal blue sweater and mustard-colored wide-wale cords. She had the tubes of a portable oxygen machine attached to her nostrils as she suffered from emphysema and could no longer be without it.

"Melanie?" Lucy said, hopping up from the table. I had arranged my visit with Oliver Owen, who delivered the animals to applewood each week and was not only the other farmhand but also her boyfriend. "You made it!"

"Hi," said Lydia in a scratchy voice. "Did you find us okay?"

I had barely said yes and sat down next to Lucy before Lydia began talking, obviously having heard from Oliver about the subject of my book.

First she blasted off a list of obstacles that face small farms. Slaughterhouses were closing because of all the red tape involved in meeting regulations: farmers who sell meat, whether retail or wholesale, are required to have it slaughtered at a plant operating under federal inspection guidelines, and the nearest of these was now hours away. Then there were customers who didn't pay for the meat they ordered. "Two or three thousand dollars might not seem like a lot to these restaurants," Lydia said indignantly, "but to one of our farmers it's a killer."

By "our farmers" she meant those who belonged to Fancy

Meats from Vermont, which was the second farmers' co-op she had run. She had owned Lovejoy Brook since 1975, after noticing its For Sale sign during a weekend visit from New York, where, after a job at *Time* magazine, she was working as a researcher for the financial columnist Sylvia Porter. She agreed to help ghostwrite *Sylvia Porter's Money Book* for a share of the royalties, and when the book hit the bestseller list in 1975 (it's still in print today, in an updated version), she made enough money to buy the ninety acres set along this gentle slope. At first she commuted, but after a few years she left New York behind and became a full-time farmer. As a teenager she had attended the Putney School in Vermont, which has a working farm and gardens and requires students to spend some of their time working in the barn and on the land. She had always, as she put it, "had a liking for farming and animals."

She also had a head for business, and she was tough, not to mention a genius at sales and marketing. She had gotten most of the restaurant customers for her original co-op, Vermont Quality Meats, simply by calling the chefs of the best restaurants in New York and persuading them to order whole animals from her. That was in 1999, when there were no other sources of high-quality meat that came with all the parts that good chefs, especially those trained in other countries, are accustomed to cooking with and consider delicacies, and she rightly guessed that they would leap at the chance to buy it from her. When she left that co-op to start over, many of the farms left with her, along with most of the restaurants she had built relationships with, and her business continued briskly. Now one of her customers was way behind in payments, and she had a plan. "I asked Benny [one of her co-op's farmers] if he'd go down and picket with a pitchfork or something and a sign saying 'X does not pay his employees.'" She gave a good-natured laugh, and I started to feel somewhat welcome if still a bit nervous.

Fancy Meats from Vermont was doing fine, businesswise, but it suffered from a slightly different version of the disconnect I felt at the meat counter. "There's a basic lack of understanding from chefs, who are far too accustomed to ordering meat from plants that can provide them with whatever they want whenever they want," Lydia said. "Few people are like David, who has made the effort to go see these places." David had told me the story of taking his kids to Vermont one spring during lambing season. To keep the newborn lambs warm, Lydia was temporarily housing them on the three couches in her living room. "Sophie thought it was the best thing she'd ever seen," he'd said.

Lydia wanted someone—me, perhaps: I was beginning to realize she understood the uses of publicity as well as she did farming—to start a newsletter that would be written from the farmer's perspective one month and the chef's the next. "There's no comprehension between the two and they could work together much better than they do," she said. "Most of the veal farmers around here have never eaten veal. Or lamb."

Suddenly she looked at me appraisingly.

"So do you take notes or what?"

"Oh, I will," I mumbled.

Lucy intervened. "Are you interested in seeing some goats?"

"Sure," I said, "but I need to do one thing first." At which point I went out to my car and wrote down everything that had just happened.

Then Lucy and I, accompanied by two big white fluffy Maremma sheepdogs named Alba and Rocco, went across the road, where a few dozen goat kids of about eight months were milling around in a labyrinth of grassy pens. The white ones were Saanens, a mellow breed that tends to give a higher volume of milk with less fat. The rest, a mixture of brown and beige and some black, were feisty Alpines, which give less milk with higher fat content. They were all adorable, especially the ones cowering in the plastic igloo-like domes set out in the grass, protecting themselves from the weather. "They hate precipitation and wind," Lucy said, patting a kid she had named Olivia in honor of Oliver. "They really like to be inside." This didn't exactly jibe with my idea of goats—admittedly based more on repeated readings of *The Billy Goats Gruff* than any actual experience. I thought of them as rakish and comical, which I confessed.

"Goats are a handful for sure," Lucy agreed. "You really have to keep an eye on them. They want to test everything, but I can see how people fall in love with them because they're so interactive. They want to be petted and to get to know you." As she said this, a brown and white kid named

Punk whose head came to just above my knees pranced up and butted my hand, and the first snow flurry of the season started to fly.

"Lydia once told me, 'Goats are a poor man's Prozac,'" Lucy said, smiling at Punk. "Not that you can be poor and have lots of goats."

It was cold outside, and there was still a little time before we had to feed the sheep, so I went in to talk to Lydia about the goats. She was in the living room, sitting at a card table piled with papers and a telephone, her back to an empty fireplace that must have been at least eight feet wide. Next to it was a wood stove that produced all the heat in the room. There was a baby grand piano ("I used to play very badly," Lydia said dryly), the three sofas where Sophie had marveled at the newborn lambs, a large table covered with reading material including several of Michael Pollan's articles about food, and a smaller table with a fax machine on it.

Because of her health, Lydia could no longer do the work of the farm as she did for many years. Instead she focused on the work of Fancy Meats from Vermont; this room was her headquarters. From the card table, she spent her Fridays calling restaurants for orders (I had heard David taking her call more than once during prep), calling back over the weekends if the chefs were too busy to talk. On Saturdays and Sundays she called the farmers in the co-op to tell them what was needed (besides meat, she distributed local eggs and cheese). On Mondays the animals were sent to one of two slaughterhouses—one in Albany, about eighty-five miles away, the

other in New Hampshire, about ninety miles away, each requiring a two-hour drive. After being slaughtered they were
left to hang (to let the blood drain out and start the aging
process, which produces flavor in the meat as muscle structure begins to break down) until Wednesday. Then Oliver
picked them up and started his long delivery route, covering
about a thousand miles in twenty hours.

But in spite of her physical remove from the daily work-
ings of her farm, Lydia's heart was clearly still very much
with the animals. She knew every detail of what was going
on. Back in the seventies, she had started Lovejoy Brook
with pigs only, but they ate so much grain at such a high
cost that she looked for other ways to sustain both the farm
and her interest. Along came the goats—"They got under
my skin pretty quick," she said between phone calls from
her post at the card table. "They're amusing, very bright,
naughty, affectionate." She also raised some chickens, cows,
and sheep, which not only kept things lively but cut back a
little on food costs. "It's really boring to be faced with four
hundred and fifty cows to milk every morning and night,"
she explained, her hand on the telephone receiver. "For example, in the typical dairy you don't do anything with the
milk. You put it in a big truck and that's the last you see of
it. We just take the milk out of the goats and feed it to the
calves and that's that. So it cuts out a lot of the boring stuff.
I think farming is capable of being very boring and repetitive
if you're doing only one thing." From the very beginning
she raised her animals without using any unnecessary anti-

biotics. "All this about growth hormones," she scoffed when I mentioned the issue. "As far as I know, no one around here does it. They never have."

Nonetheless, she made that explicit on the order sheet for Fancy Meats. When the phone started ringing, she handed me a copy. I read the prices for lambs (from one- to two-year-old "mutton" down to the little ones, which she called "hothouse" lambs), goats (five to five and a half dollars a pound), pigs (ranging from "older, fatter" animals of three to five hundred pounds, good for charcuterie, to suckling pigs weighing between twenty-five and thirty-five pounds), veal ("short fores" to hindquarters, the meatiest part of the animal), and rabbits. At the bottom was a statement of purpose: "Fancy Meats from Vermont is an association of farmers whose products are grown on small family farms, processed at USDA-inspected slaughterhouses, and delivered fresh to our customers every week. Our animals are fed primarily on milk, hay, and grain: medications are used only in life-threatening situations. We do not use growth hormones. We aim to provide the best quality meats money can buy."

Lydia was now absorbed in her phone call, and Lucy, who had been making a pie in the kitchen, suddenly appeared to ask me a question. "Do you have any wool socks?"

I did, so I put them on and we went out to feed the sheep. A little bit of snow had fallen while I was inside with Lydia. It had stopped before it had a chance to accumulate on the frost-heaved road, but it was icy outside and the light was draining out of the sky behind our destination, the sheep barn.

As we entered the old wooden building, Lucy said, "I can see why sheep are the representatives of sleep. When they're quiet this is the nicest place on the farm to be. They don't mind if you're here, but they won't want to come play with you like the goats." Inside, sheltered from the wind, it was silent. The sheep were out of sight in the other, larger section of the barn; the room we were in was called the maternity, where the lambs were born every March. Now it held feed troughs, which we filled with grain and bales of hay.

When the food was ready, Lucy slid open the enormous door between the two parts of the barn and the sheep rushed to meet her, almost knocking her down as they crammed themselves through the narrow doorway two and three at a time, pushing against one another to make it to the head of the flock, a tidal wave of freshly shorn white animals. Their eyes were gentle even as they ran for their dinner.

The hay they were eating came from nearby farms. "It's an even exchange," Lucy said. "Somebody gets their land maintained and Lydia gets hay." It was supplemented with grain because Lydia did not believe in purely grass-fed lamb from the retail point of view: she thought chefs liked the idea of it more than the actual product, which is darker and tougher than at least partially grain-fed lamb.

"You can be perfectly humane and never put your lambs at pasture," Lucy explained when I asked about that. "It's not as good for the soil, or for the landscape—sheep's hooves aerate the soil, they don't graze very much and they do graze evenly, and they poop evenly to fertilize—but this is very humane. We also give them antibiotics when they get sick."

The financial advantage of one diet versus the other was minimal: grain-fed lambs can be sold in four months while grass-fed lambs need up to ten months of growth time, but grain costs were going through the roof because so much corn was being used to make ethanol. But Lucy was more interested in talking about the environmental benefits of raising grass-fed animals.

"Grazing done well is so good for the environment and us that I think ideally people should be eating grass-fed meat only," she said as the sheep munched away. "Which in cold climates like ours includes hay during off-grazing season." Then, acknowledging the reality of feeding animals in New England winters, she conceded, "If you have to supplement, it should be with organic grain only when necessary." Whenever she finally had her own land, she planned to farm differently than Lydia—who fed her lambs non-organic grain—but she and Oliver were at Lovejoy Brook to gain experience that would allow them to make their own ideas about raising animals a reality someday, and she wasn't the least bit judgmental about Lydia's choices, in part because buying meat from a small operation like Lydia's met one of her most basic requirements.

"People should try to familiarize themselves with the source of their meat," she told me later when we continued our conversation by email. "But there's such a gap between producer and consumer that, for most people, it's hard to truly know how their food was raised and processed. Given certain conditions, cows, as one example, can pollute the waterways and atmosphere and provide us with way more meat and milk than we need. But given other conditions, cows can help us keep our soils in good shape and provide us with meat rich in cancer-fighting, bone-strengthening, mind-sharpening substances."

From the sheep barn we moved on to Lydia's cows, which lived in the upper barnyard next to the "round" barn, which was not perfectly round but twelve-sided. Lydia had designed it herself soon after buying the farm, and the two grain bins in its attic held about three tons each; along with the hay in the loft, it would be enough to get the animals through the winter.

Right now, though, we were feeding them hay, dragging bales from the barn to a sort of round metal cage that the cows could put their heads into to grab mouthfuls. Outside the cage was a pile of leftover hay from the morning meal, where three caramel-colored Jersey calves, born the previous spring, were lying, munching on whatever they could reach. Their mothers, Belle, Louise, and Rodeo, were nearby, in a small shelter a short way up the slope with Lydia's other cow, Cricket.

"There's just so much going on," Lucy said to me, petting one of the calves. "Something new every day, something you've never seen before. I really like the diversity of this farm, that there are so many animals." As if to prove her point, we made our way to the adult goats and the veal calves, who all lived in a small shedlike building next to the house that was still called the chicken coop even though it no longer served that purpose.

"I'll show you the bucks first," Lucy said, pushing the

door open. "They pay a lot of attention to the does and are also extremely disgusting. They pee on their beards as an aphrodisiac." I had trouble picturing this, so she explained. "They kind of arch their backs up into the air and scoot their back hooves closer to their front, and then bend their necks down. The penis is in what looks like the middle of their belly, so when they bend their necks like that, they can just squirt themselves."

As we entered the coop, it was clear that *someone* had been peeing in there. It was the goats' mating season, and I guess that explained the smell, which was momentarily overpowering. In a pen to my left were several Alpine does in heat, pacing around and around in the straw, waiting for their meal. A few bucks, with the aforementioned smelly, scraggly beards dangling from their chins, were across the way, staring me down inquisitively. They were, as Lucy had said, pretty disgusting, but they were funny, too, their heads bobbing up and down as they watched us stuff hay into their mangers.

In the pen next to the does were two male Holstein calves, as black and white and fluffy as stuffed animals, with huge black eyes. Lydia had bought them from another farm to raise and sell herself, and at a few weeks old, they weighed just slightly more than I did. They were wobbly and endearing, their heads too large for their bodies, and when the younger one tried to nurse on Lucy's hand, I started to feel really guilty about all the veal I'd eaten in my life, humanely raised or not.

As if she could tell what I was thinking, Lucy said, "The

way veal has conventionally been raised, I'd never eat it. They're kept in cages, they get scours, which is diarrhea, they get anemic, which is desirable for meat color." These little guys were in a pen now, but they had plenty of room to totter around on their stiff legs and play, and they spent a lot of time outside, too. "I think it's very important for the calves to run around and sit in the sun and stuff like that," Lydia had said to me, tossing out the words with a casualness that belied her obvious love of the animals.

"Do you feel bad about eating veal when you spend so much time raising them?" I asked Lucy as she fed one of the calves a big pill to help it get over the case of scours it had arrived with (which may have arisen from something as simple as travel or overeating, since calves have delicate digestive systems). She covered the pill with molasses and put it on the calf's tongue, then let the little animal suck on her hand as it swallowed, squeaking with delight while its penmate looked on.

"Some people say, 'How can you eat that?'" she acknowledged, wiping her hand on her pants. "You know from the beginning that they're going to be meat, and you try to raise them as respectfully as you can. I try to think of it as we have a good relationship. I try to treat them well and then they give me something back at the end. But everyone in general should be eating way less meat than we do. Meat should not be cheap, and if it is, you'll pay for it in other ways."

Then she introduced me to a slightly older Holstein, four-month-old Wink, who was about to be sent for slaughter. He was lying comfortably in what Lucy called the cow lounge, a roofed outdoor area joined to the coop and opening out to the cow pen. He was sweet, too, but not like the babies, primarily because he weighed about six hundred pounds, most of it gained from drinking four gallons of cow and goat milk every day—about a ton of milk over the course of his short life—along with his grain and hay. I had had no idea that veal calves were so big. I'd always imagined them as tiny babies like the two little ones, and it was harder to feel sentimental about an animal that gigantic, with a head wider than my body, who, as Lucy had pointed out, was being treated very well indeed.

"He'll be veal in a week," Lucy said, patting his rump, "but don't tell him."

Standing in the doorway between the chicken coop and the cow lounge, I wasn't much in the mood to talk to Wink or anyone else, really. It was profoundly peaceful listening to the animals rustling in the straw. Dark had fallen and my breath hung in the cold air as the goats and calves buried their heads in the mangers and began to eat. The December stars shone high in the sky above Wink's head, calm and bright.

"Rooooooooooe-deo!" "Coooome, Bellllllle!"

It was about five-thirty P.M., and Oliver and I were out in the cow pen in the pitch black, trying to persuade the cows to come down from the upper barnyard so we could milk them. Their names as he called them were long and sweet.

"Loooooooouuuuu-ise! Criiiiiiiii-cket! Rooooooe-deo!"

I was wearing sweater number three under my padded jacket, along with gloves, long underwear under my jeans, two pairs of socks, and a hat pulled as far down over my ears as I could get it. There was no sound of movement from above, just a faint lowing I thought might be coming from the small warming shed at the top of the slope.

"Rooooooooe-deeeeeeeooooooooo!" Oliver called again, stretching the word even longer than before, while I stamped my feet on the hard, uneven ground to keep off the cold. He had just come back from his delivery route and changed into an insulated coverall that covered his wiry body from neck to ankle, tucked his shaggy brown hair under a hat, turned up his collar around his beard, and headed out into the evening with me.

"They hate change," he said. "They can probably see you here."

How that was possible when I couldn't see them or anything else was unclear to me, but then, what did I know about cows? The only light came from the stars and what spilled from the tiny leaded windows of the milking barn, but maybe they had night vision.

"Roooooooooooooooe-deo!" Oliver yelled one more time, and finally, after we stood silently for a few more minutes with the cold biting at our cheeks, the cows began to traipse toward us, moving through the dark in lurches and stumbles as their hooves clattered over the frozen, snow-dusted mud ruts. They passed by me one by one, narrowly missing my feet.

We had already set up the cow-milking area in the barn

by putting sawdust on the floor in front of a wooden stanchion, essentially two vertical pieces of wood that could be
hooked together at the top to keep the cow's neck in place
so she didn't move while being milked. Behind us in two
pens were all the milk goats, about fifty of them, which we
had brought in earlier from the alleyway, a long roofed area
along the side of the coop. When we opened the side door of
the barn, the goats, much as the sheep had, poured through
in a tremendous stream, running into the main area of the
barn and then into the pens, where they made a mad dash for
the grain and fresh water I had put out for them. Now they
were fairly quiet behind us—the only sounds were of hooves
shuffling and grain being crunched—as Oliver led Louise inside.

He had put some grain in a feeder on the far side of the
stanchion; now he guided Louise's head to the feeder, and
closed the stanchion around her neck. He cleaned her teats
one by one in a soap solution, then strapped a leather belt
around her middle, hung a metal milk pan that looked like
a big tea kettle from it, and attached the milk pan's nozzles
to her udder. As she chewed her grain, he flipped a switch
to start the suction pump also attached to the milk pan, and
in a moment we heard the zinging sound of milk hitting the
metal pan. After a few minutes he felt her udder to see how
soft it had become, then gave it a little massage.

"It's to simulate the calf butting up against it to get the
milk to come out," he explained.

When Louise was done, he turned off the pump and de-
tached the nozzles from her udder. Getting a plastic bucket,

he milked out Louise by hand, stripping the last bits of milk from her with strong pulls. Then he unhooked her from the stanchion and led her out into the night, returning with Belle and setting her up the same way with the grain and the leather strap and the milk pan. While kneeling to attach the pan, he stopped for a moment and laid his head against her warm, furry side.

"Soft," he said, with the delighted look of a child. Then he added, very seriously, "You have to pay a lot of attention to cows."

It was no wonder the animals from this farm tasted so good.

While Belle was on the milking machine, Oliver mentioned that he was thinking of taking a part-time butchering job that he'd do after morning chores, "which would be great because then I'd get up early." Considering that he was already getting up at five-thirty to feed the animals and do the morning milking, this struck me as the talk of a total madman, but I held my tongue.

"I'd milk before going in," he said, "because Lucy already has another job milking at another farm."

I was officially the laziest person on earth.

The goats, by contrast, were the opposite of lazy, as I discovered when Oliver asked me to bring two of them into the small milking room while he finished up the cows.

"Just open the pen and grab two," he said. "They push a little, so watch out."

Apparently by "push a little" he meant "butt frenetically against you in barely controllable numbers." I learned this the hard way when I unhooked the gate of one of the pens and tried to release just two goats. I barely had it open a few inches when they all rushed toward me and began to shove and jostle and press their funny little faces into my stomach, trying to get out. I ended up using my body first to block them and then, after two escaped around my sides and made a sprint for the milking room, to push the rest back into the pen, literally throwing myself against them. Laughing at both the spectacle and the sheer pleasure of being surrounded by so much instinctive energy, I got a kind of contact high.

In the milking room, the two escapees had clambered up onto two small platforms, each with a small stanchion at the head, and were waiting patiently to be strapped in and given grain in their feeders. Oliver came in and set them up, attached the milk pan to the first one's teats, then went back to Belle, who was ready to be unhooked in the other room.

I was alone with two goats that were checking me out big time, wondering if I had more grain for them. To avoid their stares, I looked around the room. There was a small sink, one tiny window, a blackboard with notes about which goats were getting milked only in the morning (the goats that were dry had blue marks painted on their rumps, and whenever one came into the milking room we let it go back outside through the door to the alley). There was also a kidding chart which showed how many had been born that spring.

"There were fifty-three," Oliver said when he came back

in. "Though I'm sure not all of them lived." (To my amazement, no one seemed to have an exact goat count.)

He moved the milk pan over to the second goat and asked if I wanted to milk out the first one by hand.

When in Rome, right?

The first few pulls I made on the goat's teats, which felt rougher than I had thought they would, produced nothing. I tried to remember what Oliver had done with the cows and pulled again. Still nothing. The goat stood placidly chewing its grain, giving me a sideways look now and then.

My fingers were pretty numb with cold by this point (I had taken off my gloves for milking) so I figured that even if the sensation of milking a goat was unpleasant, I'd never know. I grabbed on and folded my fingers in around the teat one by one, pulling down hard as I did. A stream of milk shot into the stainless steel bucket.

"Nice!" said Oliver.

"I guess I was being too gentle," I replied. "I had no idea goats were so tough."

And from then on I milked with vigor. I liked the goats and their zany ways, and I liked that they were tough enough to accept a little incompetence without a fuss.

After about two hours, Oliver had finished with the cows and we had milked about twenty goats. Lucy came to the door and said she was going to take Venus, a sly beige-and-white doe, over to the chicken coop to breed her with Spartan, a buck I had seen prancing around in a pen earlier. No way was I going to miss this.

Grabbing Venus, Lucy led her out of the barn, across the

frozen cow pen, and into the coop. We pushed her into the pen with the other does and Spartan, who had already done his job with his current penmates, and shut the gate. He chased Venus around for a minute or two and then mounted her from behind for no more than a few seconds.

"Is that it?" I asked Lucy.

"Yup," she said, laughing. "You can tell because he threw his head back."

And with that we went back to the milking room, where Oliver was cleaning up. When he was done we walked out to the main room, where he had a bucket of milk for Wink.

"Do you want to try some?" he asked, dipping a cup into the bucket and handing it to me.

I sipped. It was slightly thicker than pasteurized, homogenized milk, and much silkier. Its flavor wasn't strong but had an earthy, alive quality I'd never tasted in milk before, and it was still slightly warm, though it was losing its heat by the second in the frigid air. Oliver poured the rest of the milk into a huge metal bowl for Wink, opened the barn door and called him over, and the calf and I drank together. When we had both swallowed the last drop, Wink ambled back to the cow lounge and the rest of us went to the house for our dinner.

Over an improvised pasta carbonara, which I made with eggs from the farm and store-bought bacon, Lucy and Oliver told me how they had gotten into farming. Oliver was from a military family. When his father, a colonel, retired to Alaska, Oliver followed him and got a job on a fishing boat there. Later he worked for the National Marine Fisheries Service in Massachusetts, which was where he met Lucy when she was on vacation on Cape Cod. She had grown up in a family of writers and editors in Connecticut, and after graduating from Smith in 2001 had moved to Boston to work for a nonprofit group that mentored teenage girls.

"But I never felt totally comfortable in the city," she said as we ate our pasta. She went to visit a cousin at Vermont Shepherd, a sheep farm in Putney, and everything changed in a flash. "I arrived at one A.M. in the moonlight," she recalled. "I found a pair of sandals in the barn that fit me and I had a cup of coffee that was the best coffee I ever had." She left Boston for Vermont Shepherd as soon as she could. "I was so stressed there and I never saw my roommates even though we were good friends because no one was ever at home," she said, shaking her head. "And I always just wanted to be home."

When Oliver lost his Fisheries Service job, he too fled to Vermont Shepherd. He and Lucy first contacted Lydia when they were considering taking jobs at another sheep farm and wanted information about joining her co-op and the market for lamb. She offered them work and they accepted, thinking it would be good preparation for running a farm of their own someday. "Farm families seem to thrive," Lucy told me. "I want a farm family."

How they would achieve their dream was another matter. "Getting on the land in the first place is a big hurdle," Lucy explained. "Inheriting seems to be the way to go because then you have only the taxes, though they're high, and not the mortgage. It's only going to be a more and more prevalent and pressing issue as the average age of farmers climbs—I think now it's fifty-five nationally—and those aging farmers have to consider transferring farms or selling or whatever." Leasing land was another option. As Lucy put it, "Lots of landowners want to do the 'responsible thing' with their land, but can't or won't do it themselves." In fact, just over a year after we met, she and Oliver rented land on a former dairy farm just down the road from Lovejoy Brook and turned it into a small working farm with chickens, pigs, and sheep.

But that was later. Lucy's immediate future held animals that would need to be fed and milked the next morning at six o'clock, so we said goodnight. When I pulled back the comforter on the bed in Lydia's guest room, I found a top sheet printed with sheep, Lucy's representatives of sleep. I took one look and sank in gratefully among them.

❖ Pasta with Bacon, Farm-Fresh Eggs, and Cream

6 eggs
⅓ cup heavy cream
1 cup grated Parmesan cheese
1 pound pasta (penne or spaghetti)
½ pound bacon
black pepper

1. Separate the eggs, reserving the whites for another use.

2. Mix together the eggs, the cream, and half the Parmesan cheese.

3. Cook the pasta in a large pot of boiling water. While it is cooking, sauté the bacon in a pan until it's crisp.

4. When the pasta is done, drain and mix with the hot bacon and its drippings.

5. Add the cream/egg/cheese mixture slowly, stirring so the egg coats the pasta rather than cooking in bits. When you've finished this, add the black pepper to taste and mix again.

6. Serve with the remaining cheese.

Serves 4 as a main dish.

❖ Lucy's Osso Bucco

(adapted from *The Silver Palate Cookbook*)

1 cup unbleached all-purpose flour
salt and pepper
about 6 pounds veal shanks
½ cup olive oil
4 ounces (1 stick) butter
2 medium yellow onions, coarsely chopped
6 large garlic cloves, chopped
½ teaspoon dried basil (more if fresh)
½ teaspoon dried oregano (ditto)
1 quart canned tomatoes

2 cups hard cider

parsnips, carrots, celery root, or other root vegetables,
   coarsely chopped

2 cups chicken stock

¾ cup chopped parsley

1. Season the flour with salt and pepper and dredge the pieces of veal shank. Heat oil and butter together in a large Dutch oven or casserole and sear the veal, browning well on all sides. Transfer it to a plate.

2. To the Dutch oven, add onions, garlic, basil, and oregano and cook, stirring occasionally, for 10 minutes.

3. Add tomatoes and salt and pepper to taste, and cook for 10 more minutes.

4. Add the cider and vegetables and bring to a boil. Reduce heat and simmer for another 15 minutes.

5. Preheat oven to 350 degrees.

6. Return veal shanks to Dutch oven and add stock to cover. Bake, covered, for 1½ hours. Remove lid and continue baking for another 30 minutes or so, until veal is very tender.

7. Sprinkle with chopped parsley; serve hot.

Serves 4 with big appetites, for dinner.

12

❖

Farm to Cleaver

"THERE'S COFFEE in the kitchen."

What seemed like only five minutes after I bade the sheep goodnight, Lucy was by my bed, patting me on the shoulder and saying those magic words. They were enough to make me drag my stiff body out of bed (apparently I hadn't been using my goatherding muscles much in the city). After splashing water on my face, I made a goatlike beeline for the kitchen. Lydia was there already, with a clipboard and a list of tasks to be done that day, including bringing firewood closer to the house, ready for a storm.

"There are so many things we have to do to get ready for winter," Lucy said cheerfully, pouring coffee into a thermos and handing me a cup. I glanced at the outdoor thermometer through a clear spot in the iced-over window. It read just slightly above ten degrees—a toasty eleven, perhaps.

"Let's go get the goats," she said. "It'll be warm in the milking room."

We put on our boots and extra socks and gloves and hats in the mudroom next to the kitchen and headed to the barn, while Oliver donned his insulated suit and went off in a truck to pick up the wood. It was completely dark and our feet thudded on the frozen ground. The thought of the warm milking room—where we would drink the coffee Lucy was carrying!—kept me going.

Pushing open the side door to the barn, we went inside, and I waited for a blast of warm air that did not come. The milking room was warmer, perhaps, but not warm. I guessed it was about thirty degrees in there.

"I need coffee," I whimpered. Lucy took one look at me and poured in a hurry.

As we drank from our mugs—and as I pressed mine to my face, trying to thaw my cheeks—Lucy gazed out the window pensively. "I have to say I'm looking forward to getting some real snow. If it's going to be this cold there might as well be a beautiful landscape."

And though she was going to have to spend hours out in the snow with the animals, as I looked across to the foothills in the distance, I could see her point. We downed our last sips and got to work.

By seven-twenty-five I had put out grain and water for the goats, my feet felt like blocks of ice, and I had been hit in the head by a bale of hay Lucy threw down from the loft. It seemed like a decent start to the morning. We brought in the goats—a blur of fur and hooves through the side door again—and then it was time to reel in the cows.

After another long series of calls—stubborn beasts!—we got them into their pen and Belle into the stanchion, milk bucket hanging from the leather strap around her middle. Louise came next. When there was enough milk to fill two big plastic buckets, Lucy asked me to take it over to the chicken coop and feed the calves.

Opening the barn door with my foot, I set out across the cow pen with a black bucket sloshing in each hand. A light snow had begun to fall and I crossed as quickly as I could, nodding to Wink on my way through the cow lounge. When I set the buckets down in the calves' pen they stuck their big heads into them immediately and started drinking. While they were sucking the milk down, my mind drifted to Jules, who would surely have loved them and all the other animals in the coop. In my mind, I could hear his little voice singing "E-I, E-I Donald," his version of "Old MacDonald."

Back in the barn, I discovered Lucy dashing back and forth between rooms so she could simultaneously milk cow number three and two goats.

"Do you want me to take over the goats?" I asked hesitantly. In spite of my small success the previous day, I still felt completely unqualified, but I also felt like a jerk standing around doing nothing.

"Okay," she said. "Are you sure you want to?"

I nodded and headed for the milking room. Humming along with the radio that was playing in there, I milked the goats two by two. I liked feeling them press against me when I opened the gate and watching them speed across the barn and onto the platforms. I liked the variations of their fur and the sound of the milk hitting the steel pan. I liked the goats themselves; they were silly and altogether good company.

In this way, two more hours passed, and it was nine-forty-five when we got back to the kitchen for breakfast. I could hear Lydia talking on the telephone in the living room. Lucy made oatmeal, and as the two of us sat down at the kitchen table, I asked her what she thought about the trend of eating local food. She corrected me: "I don't think it's a trend. I think it's the direction we're going and it's good for everyone."

Oliver, who had just unloaded a massive pile of wood at the back of the house, stepped in to shake the ice off his beard and eat some breakfast. When he heard what Lucy was saying, he agreed. "It's rare these days to be only one person away from knowing an animal personally, but anyone who eats our animals is affected by us." After seeing the way Oliver and Lucy treated the animals, I knew I'd much rather put my trust in farmers like them than in a corporation, regardless of whether the grain they used was organic. (As David had once put it while we watched Oliver bringing in the animals at applewood, "He walks in with carcasses over his shoulder and I think, 'I'm happy to eat that. I have no problem eating that.'")

I knew it wouldn't always be possible to be choosy—at restaurants or out on the road. There are times when you just have to eat, and if one of those times turned out to be the moment when Jules first decided to try any kind of meat, I wasn't going to stop him no matter where it came from—but I also knew what I was going to choose when I could.

Then Lydia came in. The wind was blowing fiercely outside, bringing thick clouds with it, and she was in full-on preparation mode. "I get antsy when there's a big snowstorm coming because you don't see the ground from now until April," she said. "You have to learn to have special glasses so you can see ahead to what's going to get covered by the snow sliding off the roof. Things get frozen into the ground, ladders and pails, and you don't even know the ladder's missing until you can't find it." She was also keeping an eye on the weather forecast for Oliver's deliveries on Thursday and Friday. Fancy Meats had never failed to deliver, but in really bad weather they had been delayed until Saturday, and she was hoping that wouldn't happen again.

Lucy had to feed the sheep, Oliver had to bring wood inside, and they were all running out of time for final pre-storm organization, which made me realize it was a good moment for me to head back to my family and get out of New England before the snow hit. I said my goodbyes, then stopped in the bathroom on my way out. As I was washing my hands, I noticed a framed poem hanging above the sink. Handwritten in red ink, it read:

Ah, when to the heart of man
Was it ever less than a treason
To go with the drift of things,
To yield with a grace to reason,
And bow and accept the end
Of a love or a season?

—ROBERT FROST

If this had been a gift to Lydia, the giver must have known her well. The strongest impression I'd had of her over the last few days was that she did not give up easily, whether to illness or to a winter storm.

Waving goodbye to Rocco and Alba, I raced away down the road, just ahead of the clouds, but the poem stayed in my mind all the way home. The more I thought about it, the more it seemed to apply to all of the farmers I'd met; they were all fighting against obstacles—financial, governmental, weather-related—to do the work they felt they were meant to do, and they all seemed to revel in that work despite its risks and regardless of how they had come to it. As Lucy had told me, "To be a farmer in our generation—well, one thing that hasn't changed is that you have to enjoy hard work and be willing to do it."

Later that week, when Oliver came to the restaurant to deliver the animals, we greeted each other like old friends. "It was so cool milking the goats," I said.

"You were pretty good at it," he replied, as he walked toward the basement steps with a lamb over his shoulder. "Lucy thinks you're a natural."

Sometimes the best compliments are the ones you never imagined you'd want.

I headed back into the kitchen, where David passed me carrying a big pot containing a calf's head Oliver had delivered, which I realized might very well be Wink's.

Since I no longer had any hope of avoiding the truth

about meat, I decided it was time to learn about butchering. Later that same day, when Greg had one of Lydia's lambs on the counter next to garde manger and was hacking through its bones and tendons and separating the various parts into fish boxes for later use, I paid close attention.

Greg saw me watching. "I used to own a small grocery store," he said. "I bought half cows and butchered them hanging, which is much easier."

It was?

Greg moved on from the lamb to a veal hind. Technically, it was a quarter of a calf (also possibly Wink)—basically part of a torso, a hip, and one leg, with the skin and the hoof already removed—but I imagined that many of the half-cow-butchering principles applied. First he removed the clumps of fat, which had turned an opaque whitish-yellow in the cold. Then he took out the kidney, a shiny brownish clump, and set it aside.

"Do people eat that?" I asked.

"Yes, with lemon," he said, making an ecstatic face. "But not here."

"So what are you going to do with it?"

"Maybe make it for myself for lunch." He giggled and turned back to his work.

He made a gentle slice along the veal's backbone to remove the tenderloin, which ran along the inside of the spine, and pulled the meat, a pale brick red color, away from the bone with the tip of his butcher knife. When it was free, a thick rope-like piece, he put it on a baking tray. Then he removed the strip loin, which ran along the outside of the spine and looked very similar to the tenderloin. These two pieces of meat would be stored in canola oil to seal them against the air and cooked on the grill for dinner service. The breast, which he removed next, scraping it from the ribs, was a thin, floppy piece that would be grilled that morning and ground up for meatloaf or for hash to be served at Sunday brunch.

"I once took off a veal breast, grilled it, and ate almost the whole thing," Greg said to me, rolling his eyes with a look of combined pleasure and nausea. "Ohhhhh . . ."

There were some scraping and sucking noises, the knife hitting bone and the meat coming away from cartilage, as he cut around the top of the hip to loosen the leg. Then it was off, the ball joint of the hip disengaged from its socket and exposed, a bluish-white orb in the middle of the red flesh.

Greg folded the spine into three sections with his huge hands, cracking it, and put it in a roasting pan to be used for veal stock. Then he started to break down the leg for dinner service. "You follow the white stuff," he said, pointing out the connective tissues, when I asked how he knew where to start each cut. As he ran his knife along these dividers, each muscle of flesh came loose with a moist sucking sound.

When all the meat was off the leg, he separated the knee, another, smaller ball joint. Then he went to the back of the room and returned with what I was sure couldn't possibly be a hacksaw but was, in fact, a hacksaw. He used it to cut through the shank bone so he could fit all the leg bones into the roasting pan with the spine.

In about forty minutes, he had transformed the big, unwieldy, sinewy veal hind into a stack of neatly portioned meat for dinner and a pan of bones.

Then he brought another lamb up from the walk-in, and I realized the veal had been the easy one. At least it hadn't had a head.

The lamb had been skinned, but it *did* have its head, which meant it also had eyes. And teeth. And a rigid liver-pale tongue hanging out of its mouth.

But not for long. With one stroke of Greg's big knife and one quick twist, the head was off and in the trash (there was already plenty of lamb stock in the walk-in, so this head wasn't needed). Even with just the head missing, the lamb looked less like an animal and more like meat. Its flesh was a paler pink color than the veal.

Greg began with the legs, inserting his knife at each hip joint, twisting them off one by one, and setting them aside on a baking tray. Only the hind legs had enough meat to use on the grill; the forelegs were for braises. Then he progressed as he had with the veal, removing the tenderloin and strip loins for dinner service and separating the breast meat from the rib cage with gentle swipes of his knife. The breast meat would be used to make either merguez sausage or lamb torchon for the charcuterie plate.

Inside the rib cage, when all the breast meat was off, I saw, instead of the awful sight I was braced for, a beautiful pink-ribbed tunnel in the shape of an inverted heart, almost shell-like in its translucency. It was momentarily shocking to see something of such delicate beauty in the midst of all the torn meat and bone.

Greg pointed toward the lamb legs on the baking tray and said, "Why don't you try one?" I lifted a hind leg off the tray and turned it over and over, as he had done, looking for a point of entry.

And over and over and over. Meanwhile he was slicing into another hind leg easily; it almost seemed to be coming apart in his hands of its own accord.

The two-foot-long haunch in front of me seemed impenetrable, but finally I located a line of white tissue and put my knife in. My chopping skills had improved, but this was a completely new task and I felt as if I had never held a knife before. While Greg's knife glided and barely seemed to touch the meat, I was sawing away and making ugly ridges in the smooth muscle.

"It looks so easy when you do it," I said hopelessly.

"You follow something, always," he repeated, gesturing to the bones and tissue. "It's not like you're guessing where to go." That made one of us.

Concentrating with all my might, I managed to get one leg done in about the amount of time it had taken Greg to cut up an entire animal. The knife seemed to do the opposite of what I wanted with every stroke, and I was suddenly grateful that I could buy my meat already cut up, even if there was an ounce of denial involved in doing it.

There is no denial, though, in removing goats' heads, especially when you may have recently been introduced to the goats by name in a barnyard. It isn't possible when you're trying to twist off the head as a pair of glazed-over eyes stare up at you blankly and the sounds of cracking bone, sucking meat, and whirring saw fill the room. When your hands are much too small for the job and you find them slipping and sliding and look down to see that the top of the goat's head has been opened and you can see its brains. When you give up on the twisting and instead try to bend the neck back to get the head off, and when that doesn't work, take a hacksaw to the goat's innocent young neck and slice right through it with a *skreek-skreek* noise and a grinding sound.

This "you," by the way, was me.

Having completed this task twice, I watched Greg take apart the goats I'd beheaded in the same manner he'd dealt with the lamb. Then I elected to turn my attention elsewhere because the young pig he was about to cut up weighed the exact same amount as I did, and I found it perverse. I had seen enough body parts for one morning.

But I was now on a meat high, and the next logical step was to try my hand at the grill. I had conquered fish, and I was ready for something new.

At five o'clock, after learning how to make roasted sun-chokes and cauliflower flan during prep, I presented myself to Sarah, who fixed a kind, appraising eye on me. "Okay. Let's try some temp meat."

Temp meat?

Working the grill was not even remotely like working fish. The heat level was different (read: a thousand times hotter), the order in which you cooked was different, even the vo-cabulary was different. Temp meat turned out to mean meat cooked to a specific temperature: rare, medium-rare, me-dium, well done. You let meat carry over, you braised, you stewed. There was also the vegetarian entrée. My months at the fish station, mere inches away from Sarah and the grill, seemed to have had no effect on me. I'd had blinders on when it came to everything except fish, and now I was feeling lost all over again.

"Even if I'm crazy-ass busy, I try to be ready," Sarah said, wiping her counter efficiently and stuffing her side towels inside the top of her apron, where she liked to keep them. "Whoever's on fish is running the show. I don't really know what's going on."

Which left me where, exactly?

"You're ordered in on two lambs with fish!" David called from about four feet and a world away at the fish station. Sarah bent down to her lowboy.

"What about the sides?" I asked, panicking for no reason since that night I was not responsible for anything other than staying out of Sarah's way while I watched her cook. "On fish, you do sides first."

"Meat is different," she said patiently, standing up with a stainless steel pan full of oil and pieces of lamb. "It has to rest, so you put it on the grill as soon as it's ordered in and then worry about the rest."

She plunged her gloved hand into the oil and pulled out a long lamb loin, plunked it down on her cutting board, wiped it off, and sliced off a section to cook before putting the rest back into the oil.

"Ugh. Disgusting," she said, wiping up dribbles of oil every which way and rubbing her hands on her apron. Then she salted the meat and threw it on the grill.

It was not a hugely busy night, but I felt as if my head were wrapped in cotton wool. I struggled to keep track of Sarah's movements and learn her process. When an order came in, you portioned, salted, and cooked the meat immediately, stretching your arm out over the intense heat of the grill to poke it for doneness and watching the sides for the "creep" where the color of the meat changed as it cooked.

While it was on the grill you got the sides going, by which time there was usually more meat ordered in that had to be portioned, salted, and placed on the grill, after which you poked the original piece or pieces of meat again and, when they were done, quickly removed them to the rack with tongs, which heated up the second you reached over the grill with them, so you had to snatch quickly. You checked on your sides, and when a dish was fired, you checked the corresponding portion of cooked meat sitting on the rack to see if it was still hot enough. If it wasn't, you put it back on the grill, confusingly near all the other meat that was on there by now, to warm up a bit. Before plating, you cut the meat into even slices about a quarter of an inch thick to be laid on the plate over or alongside the sides, unless you were plating a braise, which you scooped out of the pot and into a big bowl before adding the sides.

While I was watching Sarah do all this flawlessly, and cooking the occasional order myself when it wasn't too busy, David told a story about working at a restaurant—he didn't say which one—when he was high on something, back in the days when he still did that kind of thing. "It got so I was turning from the stove to the counter and I couldn't even remember what was what anymore," he said, imitating his dazed, drugged state. Only the tiny shred of consciousness I had left after sweating in front of the grill for hours, trying to switch my brain from fish mode to grill mode, stopped me from saying out loud that I felt that way *every* time I cooked, no drugs or alcohol necessary.

But there was one thing going on in the back third of the room that I understood perfectly: a barter system, meat for pastry. While the rest of us were stealing bites here and there, August and Sarah had worked out their own trade deal. She handed him pieces of meat that were too small or too well-done or had been sitting around slightly too long after cooking, and he paid her back in kind. When I expressed my total approval of this agreement, Sarah confided, "Yesterday he gave me a quart of cookies. I was quite happy last night."

Maybe I would get the knack of the grill after all.

But after a few weeks there, during which I looked longingly toward the pastry station and wondered when I might get my cookie payoff, I was no closer to being able to do it all myself. Sarah was unfailingly kind to me as I bumbled braises and duck breasts and vegetarian everything.

"How do you keep it all straight?" I asked as she flipped a few pieces of veal (I thought) and removed several others (it was actually pork). It all looked the same to me.

"Gradually, the space becomes available in your head," she said, after thinking for a minute. "Something had to happen where I just let go and stopped worrying about keeping up with the pace of things. Just because there are more people doesn't mean they're eating faster."

This made sense, and yet it was becoming clear that I did not have a grill brain. I was painfully slow and couldn't seem to reach the same state of mindless concentration I had achieved at the fish station. I was trying to do what Sarah said—think about efficiency, memorize the menu so I wouldn't waste time looking at it every time a dish was ordered in—but it didn't happen.

The weeks ticked by, and the new year was almost upon us. I arrived one afternoon to find that the window boxes in front of the restaurant had been planted with small fir trees. It was forty degrees outside, and I could tell there had been a fire in the fireplace the night before. It was my wedding anniversary, and I intended to spend the evening cooking and then leave a bit early with some delicious snacks to take home to Noah.

But first, more confusion at the grill. That night my main problem was pork—specifically, getting my slices of pork to lie neatly on the mound of braised pork and green lentils I had made in the center of the plate. I was splashing juices everywhere, and as Sarah cleaned up my mess she suggested, "Challenge yourself on the next plate. Fewer motions."

"Okay," I said.

But my spoon was unsteady and I scooped and splashed even more. The slightest hesitation threw the whole process off, and once that happened it was hard to right things again.

And that was just the plating. My visit to Lydia's farm

had clarified my ideas about what meat to eat and why, but it had not made me feel better about cooking meat at the restaurant. It had not made me feel better about plunging my hand into a pan of oil over and over again. Or stretching my forearms across the grill to reach something at the back that was cooking in a place so hot I had to take my wedding ring off before reaching for it or the ring got so hot that it left a red mark on the flesh underneath. Pretty much nothing was going to make me feel better about that. I was tired of the grill, and as Jules had taken to saying when he was mad about something, I didn't want it.

I begged off early, pleading marital festivities at home. On my way down the block in the freezing cold, loaded with cheeses and pâtés and other celebratory food David had heaped on me and refused to let me pay for, I realized two rather amazing things. I had been married eight years. And I missed the fish station.

❖ No-Grill Pork Tenderloin with Balsamic Vinegar

(loosely adapted from Marcella Hazan)

2 tablespoons butter
1 tablespoon vegetable oil
2 pork tenderloins (about 1½–2 pounds total)
salt
freshly ground black pepper

½ cup good red wine vinegar

3 bay leaves (optional)

1. Put a heavy pot (enameled works well) on a burner over medium heat and add the butter and vegetable oil.

2. Once the butter foams (do not let it turn brown), add the meat and brown well on all sides, turning it to get good browning everywhere. Turn down the burner to medium low and salt and pepper the meat.

3. Add the balsamic vinegar and the bay leaves if you're using them. Loosen any crusty bits from the bottom of the pot, bring the liquid to a simmer, then cover the pot tightly and cook for about 20–30 minutes, turning the meat occasionally.

4. When the meat is tender (test with a fork) remove it from the pot, keep it warm, and let it rest.

5. Add ½ cup of water to the juices in the pot, plus a bit more balsamic vinegar if you wish, then scrape any remaining bits from the bottom, turn up the heat, and reduce the liquid.

6. Slice the meat and serve with the reduced pan juice.

Serves 4 as a main dish.

13

❖

Out to Sea

By MIDWINTER I accepted my fate and abandoned the grill for good. David had once told me that different personalities go better with different stations, and by now it was clear that I should throw my lot in with the fish. Which meant, of course, that I needed to learn how to handle whole fish, not just pre-cut portions of flesh ready to hit the frying pan. I started small, with fifty sardines that glistened beneath my fingers like sleek jewels. One cold afternoon David sent me down to the walk-in to bring up a box of them, and when I saw them shining on their bed of ice, I felt inspired. I had always leapt at the chance to order sardines in restaurants, but never dared to buy them whole at the fish store for fear of ruining them with my ignorance. I knew so little about cleaning fish that I couldn't imagine where to begin. (And being married to Noah, who had gutted every one of those fish he caught on his spear as a kid, didn't help me learn since he always stepped in when fish needed cleaning.)

Bringing the box into the kitchen, mindful of Sarah's advice to challenge myself, I asked David to show me how to clean just one sardine before leaving me on my own with the remaining forty-nine.

Following his example, I placed one on my cutting board (which I had stuck to the counter with wet paper towels like a pro) and began to scrape off the scales, little incandescent medallions, with the back of a small knife. They flew everywhere as I swept the knife in the opposite direction of their growth, covering my counter top with a mother-of-pearl sheen. Underneath them, the fish skin was unexpectedly gorgeous, like silver leather shot through with gold on the sides, fading into a shimmering blue-black ridge along the back.

When all forty-nine were scaled, I slit them along their bellies one by one and pulled out the insides, a small tangle of red and brown and green. Once prepped, they would go into a fish box and into the lowboy at the fish station. They would be served that night, sautéed whole with Meyer lemon jam and caper butter.

"Where did these come from?" I asked David as I gutted. "Are they farmed?"

Fish farms are one of the ways in which we're trying to compensate for the overfishing that has already taken place in all of the world's oceans, but they're an imperfect solution. As Charles Clover writes in *The End of the Line,* "Farmed fish have the same problems amplified by unnatural confinement that intensively bred livestock do. They need drugs to treat illnesses and pesticides to kill parasites. They lead brief, sedentary lives like other domesticated creatures. They are fed with ground-up smaller fish, which are often themselves overfished. This concentrates the pollution present in the sea in the fatty tissues of the farmed fish (as eating smaller fish does naturally in the flesh of larger, longer-lived predatory fish). . . . For this reason the conservation of wild fish is a human health issue as well as an environmental one." Or, as Mark Bittman puts it, "Farm-raised fin fish are really the cage-raised chickens of the sea."

At the moment it's generally agreed by experts like these that clams and mussels and oysters, which live on plankton and can be harvested without damaging the environment, are just about the only good farmed options. American tilapia and a few other fish that don't eat wild-fish feed and can be raised inland, where they won't harm coastal vegetation, are also okay, though issues of flavor come up with them.

At applewood, David buys only wild fish that have been caught sustainably, subscribing to Clover's idea that "given the choice, most of us would prefer to eat wild fish. So it is rational to consume wild fish in a way that promotes their continued abundance." Accordingly, David's answer to my question about the sardines was: "They're from the Mediterranean Sea, not farmed." When I asked why they came from so far away, he explained that when it comes to "promoting abundance," local is less important to him than sustainable because the destruction of ocean life and habitats is already so advanced. He was more willing to buy seafood from Alaska or Spain that had been fished responsibly than seafood that came from a shorter distance away but was overfished or in danger of becoming so, or that had a high level of by-catch—the name for fish that are accidentally swept up with target fish and then thrown back into the water, usually dead. (That said, applewood is also always looking for good local food, and soon after this conversation David began buying sardines from Maine rather than from the Mediterranean.)

Every day David gets an email from his fishmonger that lists, much in the manner of the Angello's weekly email, which fish is available, where it's from, and how it was caught. Generally speaking, hook and line is the most commonly used environmentally friendly way of fishing. It allows fishermen to keep only the fish they're after, and to throw back anything else immediately, while it's still alive. Traps and pots used to catch lobsters, shrimp, and bottom-dwelling fish are also considered fairly safe, though they can cause some habitat damage, and the same goes for gill nets, which have different sizes of netting to allow fish other than the targeted species to swim through unharmed (though gill nets do produce some by-catch and can entangle marine mammals and sea turtles). Worst in terms of both environment and by-catch are methods like trawling and dredging, which literally tear up the ocean floor and also catch a lot of unwanted fish, and purse seining, which involves scooping out whole schools of fish at once. (Purse seining was the method that provoked such public outcry about tuna because so many dolphins were swept up in the netting with schools of tuna.)

If David wants to order fish on a given day, after checking the email he calls the fishmonger's outgoing message machine, which gives him last-minute updates on weather and fishing conditions that might change availability. Then he cross-checks any fish he wants to buy against the online Seafood Watch list put out by the Monterey Bay Aquarium, and makes his order.

Even though David buys from all over, a great deal of applewood's fish, depending on the season, comes from fairly close by. As spring rolled in and the weather finally began to warm up, I drove to Barnegat Light, New Jersey, to bring my fish obsession to its natural conclusion: a day on the open sea.

On the Sunday of Memorial Day weekend, I headed south to the very tip of Long Beach Island. I had made arrangements to stay in a motel right near the docks and get picked up at two-forty-five A.M. on Monday by Kevin Wark, a Barnegat Light native and a dayboat gill-net fisherman, who supplied fish to the company applewood ordered from. What was one more sleepless night? After a dinner of local fish and chips, I went to bed at ten, my green galoshes at the ready by the door of my motel room.

At exactly two-forty-five, as I was pulling them on (I had already swallowed my Dramamine and put on some wristbands that were supposed to prevent seasickness through pressure points), there was a knock at the door. I opened it to find Kevin, big and broad and tan with shaggy brown hair, sun-bleached blond on the top layer, that made him look far younger than his forty-five years. He was wearing jeans and a navy blue sweatshirt, along with a pair of sunglasses on top of his head. It was pitch-black outside, but I took the glasses as a hopeful sign.

"Hey, nice to meet you," he said, grabbing my duffel bag. "My truck's right outside."

After a quick ride in his pickup, we arrived at the docks and walked out a lamp-lit dock to his boat, a forty-two-foot lobster boat called the *Dana Christine*. "I named it after my little girl," he explained, hopping down to the deck and holding out his hand to me. "She's nine." As I jumped on after him he continued happily, "It's very seaworthy. It can take some weather and you don't have to worry about it coming apart. It can take more than you can." (In retrospect, this was a statement to which I should have paid closer attention.)

In the small cabin, I wedged myself onto the narrow bench under the side window and Kevin started flipping switches on pieces of equipment. There was a round green radar screen with concentric circles that looked like a target and showed everything within about six miles of the *Dana Christine*. There was also another kind of radar, black and white, called a chromoscope, that showed the depth of the ocean. And there were various other gauges and needles that monitored the engine and the gas tank. We were going to steam fifty-two miles out to sea to the monkfishing grounds where Kevin and Mike, his deckhand, had put out their nets the day before. We had to leave early to have enough time to reach the fishery, pull in the nets, get back to the dock, and unload the fish before the marina closed at five o'clock that afternoon. The trip out would be fast in order to get to work as soon as possible in case there was lost gear or we had to visit more than one fishing ground. "We're going to burn a gallon of fuel for every mile," Kevin sighed. "And right now that costs me about eight hundred dollars." The return trip would be slower to save fuel. A gallon per mile sounded like a lot of fuel to me, but actually, when compared with the amount of fuel burned per ton of fish caught by a large-scale commercial fishing boat, it's very little. According to the Sea Around Us Project, which investigates the impact of fishing on marine ecosystems, small fishing boats catch about twenty-four million metric tons of fish per year using between one and three million metric tons of fuel, while big ships not only use far more fuel (fourteen to nineteen million metric tons) to get a similar amount of fish (twenty-nine million tons) but also use destructive trawlers and produce ten to twenty million tons of by-catch.

Kevin's monkfish permit, issued by the National Marine Fisheries Service (NMFS), allowed him twenty-seven "days at sea" with a limit of three thousand pounds of monkfish per trip. If we didn't get back in time to unload the fish that afternoon, he'd have to unload it the next morning, losing a day of fishing and the income from the fish he might have caught. One of the arguments against this system, which many environmentalists want changed, is that it encourages fishermen to fish very aggressively on their few permitted days, which is hard on the fisheries and can result in large numbers of fish—anything over the weight limit—being thrown back into the water as by-catch. For Kevin, it also had other shortcomings. "If it's slow you don't want to go out there and waste your time," he explained. "You'll kill yourself financially. It's a real juggling act to try to hit everything just right, and if you make a mistake you're screwed." He spent the dead winter months, February and March, when no fish were running, making sure his nets and his boat and his radar were well-prepared. "You just spend buckets full of money trying to fix everything that you possibly think's going to fail. You just rehab. It's a war of attrition during the season."

Just then Mike appeared in the cabin door. He was forty, but, like Kevin, looked younger, and he had curly red hair. They had known each other most of their lives, and Mike had worked for Kevin for fourteen years. Mike had untied the boat when he got on, and after introducing himself quickly, went down to the sleeping area under the prow, where he stowed his lunch in a corner and then curled up under a sleeping bag on one of the thin mattresses to get some rest.

"There's no bathroom on board," Kevin said cheerfully as the boat made a sputtering sound and moved away from the dock. "If you need to go, just tell me and I'll give you a bucket." And then we were off, out into the vast ocean.

When we reached open water, Kevin gunned the engine and we started clipping along at sixteen knots (about seventeen miles) an hour. Through the window next to my perch, I could see nothing but blackness—I couldn't even tell where the sky ended and the water began—punctuated occasionally by the bobbing light of a buoy. The stars were spread all across the sky, and the purring of the engine combined with the sound of the boat pushing through the water was incredibly soothing.

Out on the water, Kevin became talkative, and I was glad to listen. "I built my first boat when I was thirteen," he said, checking the green screen, which now looked intergalactic, pocked with blips that showed buoys and other boats. "If you needed money, you went out," he added. "We sold crabs in the neighborhood to the tourists, we sold minnows, and we sold clams to my grandfather. He had a clam house. My dad was an electrician, not a commercial fisherman, but we always had boats and I always knew I was going to go fishing. I remember being a little kid seeing the commercial boats go by and thinking, 'I've got to get on that and see what's going on.' That's what we did after school, we went out in the bay. I have an older brother who was a clammer for years. I have a little brother that fishes. There was no transition for me. It just seemed like that's what we were born to do."

He was quiet for a minute, then spoke again. "I think we're a dying breed, though. I don't think there will be another generation of fishermen. You don't see too many young people getting into the business. It's so expensive to get into, and permits are so expensive, anywhere from thirty-five to a hundred thousand dollars, depending on the size and horsepower of the boat. It was three hundred sixty-five thousand dollars for an unequipped boat I saw in Maine last summer."

I thought of Charles Clover's question about the dying fishing industry: "Can we afford to be sentimental about fishermen if the price of having too many of them is the destruction of fish and the wonders of the ocean, which we are only just beginning to understand?" One of the people Clover interviewed answered him this way: "I grew up in an area of dairy farms, with small towns scattered every few miles apart . . . Now agribusiness owns more than ninety percent of the farms and the little towns are either empty or gentrified by people who commute an hour each way to the city to work and shop. A rich interesting culture was lost, and no one blinked." His argument was that the same was happening in fishing communities, and from what Kevin was saying, he clearly agreed. I wondered out loud where we would get our fish if that happened.

"You're going to get your fish from foreign countries," he said matter-of-factly. "The National Marine Fisheries Service crushes the domestic fisheries, and the imports just fill the vacuum. The more they regulate us, it just creates opportunities for others."

I started to protest about overfishing and disappearing species, and to my surprise, Kevin didn't disagree. For someone who seemed antagonistic toward what he called "the fish regime," Kevin has spent an enormous amount of time working with regulators to develop rules that preserve both fish and the livelihood of fishermen. He's testified before Congress and is a member of the local division of his fisheries council, and he's helped scientists with their stock-assessment projects. As he told me, "I've always been drug into it, first just to sustain myself and then they get to know you." And even though the bureaucracy sometimes drove him nuts, he wasn't against it. "We need rules, but we need smart rules that make sense—steady supplies, smaller amounts. Good science is key to all of this, and moderation is key, no doubt about it, but you have to make the industry viable or [fishing's] not worth doing. It's a fine line."

He wanted to make a profit, but he paid attention to more than just money. "We all like conservation, and we all want to have fish for tomorrow. We don't want to fish ourselves out of a job. We're the barometers of the ocean. If we see that we can't catch anything we know we're in trouble." Like Richard or Lucy or Elizabeth MacAlister wanting to preserve land, Kevin wanted to preserve the ocean, partly because he made his living from it but also because he was part of a community supported by fishing that he saw being slowly decimated. "Domestic production is being lost slowly but surely between overfishing and habitat degradation," he said. "But there are some species that have made comebacks, and the regulations don't take the restaurant business or the marketing into consideration. How can you have a product for a month and then it disappears?"

This seemed to be another version of what Joe Angello had said about labeling. As with produce, applewood could take whatever fish a guy like Kevin brought in, but many other restaurants and stores couldn't because their menus and sales setups didn't change every day. This left small day-boat fishermen like Kevin at a disadvantage. More than any other part of the food chain I'd seen, fishing seemed imbalanced when it came to the needs of the consumers, the environment, and the producers (fishermen, in this case). It's been estimated that if we don't reverse overfishing trends very soon, the ocean will be virtually out of fish by 2048, and according to the United Nations Food and Agriculture Organization, about seventy-five percent of fish species are already either overfished or "fully exploited," and yet we consumers continue to demand vast quantities of fish even as fishermen—like farmers—sometimes struggle to stay solvent. Standing at the wheel of the *Dana Christine,* Kevin suddenly looked awfully isolated.

We had been on the water for about two and a half hours by now—Mike was completely crashed in the sleeping area—and I was getting dozy. Behind us the stars still glowed, even as ahead of us the sun was starting to rise, brushing pink and orange streaks along the horizon. "I'm going to go down and grab a nap," Kevin said. "You can sleep, too, honey."

And with that, I dropped my pen and pad to the floor, lay down on the bench, and passed out.

When I woke up, it was broad daylight and we had dropped anchor. I wasn't quite sure who had been driving the boat while I, and presumably Kevin, slept—perhaps Mike had taken a turn—but now it was seven-thirty A.M. and Kevin and Mike were putting on their big boots, plastic pants, and hooded rain jackets in preparation for getting splashed out on deck. The boat, which had been chugging along smoothly before my nap, was now pitching violently from side to side at almost ninety degree angles to the water.

"I think I'll take you up on that bucket," I said to Kevin,

trying to sound very calm, as he tossed me a pair of plastic pants. He went outside to help Mike begin to bring in the net, which they located via a GPS attached to a buoy attached to a ground rope that led down to the net, and I went down to the sleeping area with the plastic pants and the bucket. As I struggled into the pants, my stomach pitched along with the boat. I barely got them on before I threw up.

Goodbye, Dramamine.

Then, because I was feeling what would turn out to be very temporarily half-decent, I headed out on deck to watch Kevin and Mike bring in the fish. After all, this was why I had come along. And what could be better when you're feeling sick than seeing a lot of dead fish?

For a while, things went along (forgive me) swimmingly. Perched on the edge of the boat so I could throw up right into the water (I'm all for convenience), I watched Mike and Kevin begin to pull in their net by winding it around a large spindle, called a drum, on deck. The net was large mesh so smaller fish could swim through, and it lay along the ocean floor, held by weights, until they brought it up. ("You can fish anywhere from ten to forty fathoms," Kevin told me, "depending on what kind of boat you have and how much moxie you got.") In it were many monkfish and an occasional skate, which was Kevin's by-catch (skate are considered overfished, though catching certain species is not entirely banned by the NMFS). In order to empty the net, they had to stretch it open with one hand and wrestle each fish out of its web with the other. When the fish were free, Mike and Kevin threw them into large coolers lining the side of the boat.

I've never particularly liked to eat monkfish, and now I felt totally justified. They were hideous, mud-colored beasts with huge heads, big lumpy tails, and pretty much nothing in between except for a weird little fin on each side that looked as if it had gotten caught midway through an evolutionary change from swimming to walking. They may have been called the poor man's lobster, but they sure didn't look like it, and it wasn't just my queasy stomach making me feel that way. Each fish was about one-third tail, and the rest of it seemed to be its awful head.

Kevin brought one over to where I was sitting, half on the side of the boat, half on the deck in an effort to find a position that would make me feel even slightly less terrible. "Check out its mouth!" he said enthusiastically. And though the last thing I really wanted to do at that moment was look deep inside a disgusting, slimy creature, I was literally painfully aware that if I didn't do it then, I was probably not going to feel well enough to do it later on.

Kevin pried open its mouth with some effort; the fish was clearly not interested in displaying its jagged little teeth for me. Steeling myself, I turned toward it and upon looking in discovered an intricate pale-pink-and-white architecture supporting all the ugly flesh and skin. The monkfish's huge head, as wide as the whole fish was long, was all mouth. Its interior, used to catch and hold prey as big as the fish itself,

was clean and fresh looking and arched at the top like a miniature cathedral ceiling.

"It's beautiful," I said, surprised and thus momentarily
distracted from the roiling in my stomach.

"You gotta watch out for the teeth, though," said Kevin.
"Watch this." Mike came over and put his hand, sheathed in
a thick rubber glove, into the pink space that lay beyond the
rows of long sharp teeth. The monkfish instantly snapped
on, digging deep into the glove. It took both of them to pry
its mouth open again, after which Kevin threw the fish into
a cooler and they went back to bringing up lengths of net.

After this little party trick was over, I excused myself and
retreated to the cabin, where for the next hour and a half I
lay on the floor with a plastic bucket, throwing up every few
minutes, long past the point when it seemed humanly possible to throw up any more, and staring at the ceiling between eruptions. Kevin and Mike went about their business
as though they did not have a limp author sprawled on their
floor in huge plastic pants (great not only for fishing but for
lying on a wet surface in agony). Every once in a while Kevin
came in to check on me or look at a radar screen.

"Don't feel funny, honey," he said, as I retched into the
bucket mid-conversation. "You're doing great."

This appraisal seemed fairly generous, seeing as I hadn't
even been able to sit up in recent memory, but apparently
Kevin considered my condition a mild case.

"You don't want to know the things I've seen out here,"
he said on his fourth or fifth visit. "I've had people projectile

vomiting out the cabin door. I've had cops crawling around on their hands and knees demanding I take them back to land when we were four hours out. I know a thousand captains I wouldn't go out with. I was surprised you didn't get sick sooner." I took this as the comfort it was intended to be and turned back to my bucket.

We went over to one more fishery so Mike and Kevin could fill their allotted three thousand pounds of catch. Then they gutted all the fish, close to three hundred of them, out on deck. I rallied just enough to peek out the cabin door, still lying on my side, to see how they did it—slit the stomach, pull the guts out, put them in a bucket, dump it in the water when you're done. Then Kevin turned the boat homeward. It was eleven o'clock in the morning and there was nothing left to do but motor slowly for shore.

"We'll probably gross about three thousand dollars on this trip," he said. "That's a good day, no lost gear. Seven hundred and fifty pounds of fish and we'd break even. We're the top-producing small boat on the East Coast—I caught three hundred fifty thousand pounds of fish last year, and some years I catch over four hundred thousand." (In addition to monkfish he fished for bluefish and weakfish, among others.)

Even in my compromised state, I marveled at these numbers. Kevin had more to tell me. "There's a lot of luck involved and a lot of hard work. You have to have the fortitude and know where to go and have the gear ready. And the amount of hell, what time you're getting up—we're not going out there for fun. Some of those rides you're just beat to hell before you get there."

For now, though, the hell part seemed to be over. "We'll use half the fuel we did going out," he said from his captain's chair, which seemed yards above my position on the floor, "and it will take twice as long. You'll feel better once we get moving again, and really, don't feel funny, honey. Even Mike got sick for the first few weeks he was out here."

Mike, who had come in to get his lunch—the mere thought of someone eating made me throw up into the bucket one last time—nodded his head. He was clearly the silent partner. Then, looking at me thoughtfully, Kevin asked, "Are you going to write about this?"

It was a long ride back. We pulled into the docks where the fish would be processed around four o'clock. Though I had, as Kevin promised, recovered considerably in the interim, my knees were shaking when I stepped onto the dock.

"Feels pretty good, doesn't it?" he said with a big smile.

"Yup," I said. With the ground beneath my feet, I felt about twenty pounds lighter and inestimably happier. Kevin drove me back to my car, and I managed to say goodbye without throwing up. As I got into the driver's seat, I wondered if I'd ever eat fish again.

It wasn't for a few more hours, until I was on the New Jersey Turnpike headed home, that I could contemplate eating even anything that wasn't fish. I pulled over and bought water and a box of saltines, and said a little prayer of thanks when the first bite stayed down. Once I was on the road again, I could think a little more clearly about what I'd seen that day. We don't all get a daily email with information about our fish as David did (though maybe that's a business someone should start), and once I was home he was the first person I went to with my remaining questions.

"'Dayboat' is not automatically good, there's more to it than that," he told me when I cornered him in a quiet moment at the restaurant the following week. "Dayboat really just means that the fish hasn't been frozen overnight; you can still catch cod and skate on a dayboat." (Atlantic cod is severely overfished.) He was right, of course, but at some point you have to make choices. Gill nets are considered environmentally damaging by the same people who put out the list David consults when buying fish, but applewood buys from a small Alaskan salmon harvester that uses them successfully, with a very low percentage of by-catch, in a sustainable fishery.

And dayboat fishing had other attractions as well, the same attractions as supporting small farmers who were helping to keep their communities vibrant. "Buying local really helps the mom-and-pop and subsistence fishermen," Kevin had told me on the way out to the fishery. "We have a forty-two-foot boat and we're taking everything out with our own two hands. That's not the kind of operation that's going to sweep the ocean clean. We've proven that the monkfishery is very sustainable, but it's really hard."

When I checked on this later, I discovered that after the monkfish population declined precipitously in the 1980s and 1990s, the NMFS put a management plan in place that allowed some fishing again by 2003; as of 2009, Atlantic monkfish were considered fully recovered and also a great fisheries-management success story. Meanwhile, the Monterey Bay Aquarium's Seafood Watch tells consumers to avoid monkfish largely because of the methods typically used to catch it—bottom trawls and gill nets.

When Kevin and I spoke some time after our boat trip, I mentioned this conflicting information. "I saw the other day someone had monkfish on the unsustainable list," he said, an edge of frustration in his voice. "I see all kinds of wrong stuff out there." And while it's true that he has a vested interest in considering monkfish sustainable, it's also true that he wants to make sure they don't disappear, so he fishes as responsibly as possible with nets that meet NMFS specifications for mesh size and with a reduced number of days at sea that limits how much he can catch; there's a big difference between his operation and a big commercial trawler. "The Fisheries Service is trying to bring all the species back," he had said when we were out on the water. "We'll get there eventually. I'm sure of that. These fisheries have to be rebuilt." I heard Richard in my head—"These little farms have to be farms again"—and figured that if Kevin had reason to be optimistic, so did I.

As it turned out, I had more than just fish to be hopeful about. When I walked into our apartment after my day on the

Dana Christine, still slightly woozy and convinced I would have to live on saltines for the rest of my life, but bursting with seafaring tales to tell Noah, he got his news in first.

"Guess what Jules likes?"

"What do you mean?" I said suspiciously. "Did you buy him a skateboard?"

"No." Long, very pregnant pause. "Sausages."

"You mean like meat sausages?"

"Yeah," said Noah. "These little dry turkey sausages. Meat sausages."

And just like that, I loved food again.

We had had signs that Jules's stubbornness in the eating department was weakening. The first one had come about a month before I went fishing, at another child's birthday party. I was talking to a friend when I saw Noah approaching from across the room with a stricken look on his face.

"Is something wrong?" I asked, scanning the room for a heap of broken child or some other disaster.

"Jules just ate a bite of my pizza," Noah choked out.

My friend gave him a peculiar look. "What do you mean ate a bite?" I asked.

"I mean he bit down on my slice and took some of it in his mouth and didn't spit it out," Noah explained carefully, like one biologist telling another about the eating habits of a rare species.

"I think I'll go get a cupcake," the friend said, leaving us to our baffled happiness. Having been burned before (remember his brief fling with salami?), I decided to take this possibly monumental development in stride.

But whether it was because I refused to get excited or just because it was spring and things were thawing all around us, that bite of pizza turned out to be, if not the start of something big, at least the start of something different. In a single week that April, Jules tried wax beans (raw, of course, so they were crunchy), corn on the cob, and fresh green peas straight from the pod. When we went to the grocery store, he sat in the cart pointing at things he wanted to try, just the way all the books had said he was supposed to when he was one. He didn't eat most of them, but he had suddenly become aware of the variety of food that existed, and he was interested in it. Meat of any kind was still an issue, which was why Noah was so excited about the turkey sausages on Memorial Day weekend, but we were finally on our way.

When we took Jules to the pediatrician for his regular checkup and told her he'd started trying new foods, she said, "That's odd. Most kids do it the other way. They eat anything until they're two and then start cutting back." (This was the same doctor who, when we reported that Jules's first word was "No," looked at us pityingly and said "You're in trouble.") Yes, it was odd, but oddness was what we had come to expect from him where food was concerned. Cautiously at first, we began to assume he would try something every once in a while, which was more than enough for us.

New spring produce was abundant in the kitchen again, too. "It's starting!" David said happily the same week that Jules first ate beans, peas, and corn. "It's so exciting! You get so tired of all the yellows and browns and then everything goes green all at once." Something was in the air, and it smelled like new life. As the season shifted, so did the lives of everyone at applewood. Greg got married, Sarah decided to move back to her native Pittsburgh with her fiancé and become a private chef, and David hired a new grill man, who also happened to be a documentary filmmaker. One afternoon I arrived to find Laura hauling Sophie and Tatum's futon bed out of the office. They hadn't slept on it for months, since David and Laura had hired a babysitter to pick them up after school and stay with them at home until one parent or the other could get there, but this last vestige of the early days at applewood had lingered.

"I'm so happy to get this thing out of here," Laura said. The office was strictly an office at last (though the sheep tea party mural remained). Before long, Laura and David also hired enough part-time chefs and floor staff to allow each of them to take a night off every week and spend it with their kids. On those days the girls frequently appeared on their bikes after school, around the time of family meal, to say hi to whoever their working parent was.

"Wow, they're really growing up," I said to David after one of these visits, as he was showing me how to julienne green apples for a slaw with lime juice and parsley.

"I know," he said, a nostalgic look in his eye. "I have this image of Sophie in her highchair, when she had barely started eating food, with a huge venison chop in her hand." And for the first time, the idea of Jules with a venison chop didn't seem entirely outlandish to me.

❖ Pan-Roasted Sardines with Caper Butter

6 whole sardines
3 tablespoons canola oil
salt
½ stick butter
¼ cup capers

1. Scale and gut the sardines. Place one fish on a cutting board and, starting at the tail and working your way up to the head, use the back of a small knife to scrape off the scales by running the knife against the direction in which they grow. Flip the fish and repeat on the other side, then repeat with each fish.

2. To gut them, slit open the stomach, pull out the innards (they should come out easily, essentially in one yank), and discard.

3. Heat the canola oil over medium-high heat in a frying pan big enough to hold all the sardines.

4. When the oil is hot, salt each sardine on both sides, put them in the pan, and turn the heat down to medium. Let them cook, untouched, for about 5 minutes, then flip them and let them cook for about 3 minutes.

5. Remove the sardines to 2 plates (3 to a plate), turn down the heat to low, and put the butter in the pan. As it melts, scrape up any bits left in the pan. When it's melted, add the capers and sauté for a minute or so.

6. Spoon the caper butter over the sardines and serve with greens and a wedge of lemon.

Serves 2 as an appetizer.

❖ Seasickness Cure

1 box saltine crackers
1 bottle sparkling water

1. Open box.
2. Open bottle.
3. Eat one tiny bite of cracker alternating with one tiny sip of water, making sure to remain near an open window or, if possible, an exit to the outdoors.
4. Repeat. Repeat. Repeat.

Fills one very empty stomach, little by little.

14

❖

Sweetness and Light

"AUGUST NEEDS HELP."

I had been waiting to hear these words since my first day in the kitchen.

What I said in response was: "Okay, sure."

What I thought was: "Me? Go to the place with the cookies and chocolate and sugar and candied everything? Yes!"

I had been making one last halfhearted attempt at the grill (after my day on the *Dana Christine*, my intoxication with the fish station had faded), but the weather was warm now and it seemed like a good idea to be as close as possible to the homemade ice cream. Back I went to pastry, a part of the room I had only passed through before, and within minutes I was blissfully surrounded by miniature pecan tart crusts and flour. As at the grill, I was completely disoriented and lacked the vocabulary to have a conversation about what I was supposed to be doing. Unlike at the grill, though, the lowboy in front of me contained—instead of tenderloins submerged in oil and one-pound chunks of butter—chocolate sauce and mascarpone cream, things I understood instinctively in a way I could never understand raw meat. It also held the dough for the tart crusts, which August pulled out and placed on the counter. He showed me how to roll it out on the floured countertop and cut circles in it with—of course—a quart container.

"So then do I use this . . . this pastry knife to get them off?" I asked hesitantly.

"Yeah, yeah. Call it whatever. It doesn't matter," August said, picking up the long flexible blade, rounded and blunt on the end, and sweeping it under one of the circles. Then he pressed the dough into a little fluted tart tin about two and a half inches wide, tamping it down gently with his fingers until it filled the space nicely.

"Then trim it, like this," he said. With one deft swoop of the nameless tool, he cut the drooping edges off the crust. Turning back to the crepes he was making to fill with caramelized pears and ricotta and serve with cinnamon ice cream and cranberry sauce, he said in the nicest possible tone, "It doesn't have to be fast or anything."

Which, though probably not true, was a good thing to hear because I spent the next five minutes completely botching the first crust I tried to put into a tiny tart tin. Every time I pressed it, it tore, until I finally gave up on that one and rolled out the dough again to cut more quart circles. For every batch of three tarts, I messed one up irrevocably. The dough was too thick, or I tore it, or I trimmed off too much when I was trying to swoop the knife around the edge of the tin. Somewhere behind me, I could hear Sarah saying "short ribs with kale and black bean–bacon purée," and it sounded like a foreign language. It took me almost thirty minutes to make twelve very small tart crusts.

But August was nothing but grateful. He had to make five new desserts before dinner service began. (Unlike the savory food, desserts were almost all made ahead of time and then assembled when they were ordered, so dinner service itself wasn't hard, but the hours leading up to it were.) "Thank you so much for your help," he said.

"You have to make all of these?" I asked, looking at the list he had taped up. It read: "Pecan tarts, fruit compote, chocolate soufflés, crepes, orange cream, quince purée, pineapple compote, crème brûlées, butterscotch, cherry soup."

"Oh yeah," he replied, scratching the top of his head through the Che Guevara baseball cap he always wore in the kitchen. "But it's easy. At one of my old jobs I had to do five hundred desserts a night, pre-theater, dinner, and post-theater. I had to get to work at five A.M."

"No wonder you seem so unworried," I said as I popped a caramelized macadamia nut into my mouth. "I would be freaking out."

"Oh, I have a hidden temper," he said impishly, plating his crepe dessert for the servers to try. Watching him stick a shortbread star to the plate with a gob of marzipan and place a scoop of cinnamon ice cream on the star, I found that hard to believe.

August was twenty-six and had started out as a line cook in Florida at the age of seventeen. Then he had applied to be a bartender on the Carnival Cruise line because he thought it would be fun and he'd get to travel. When that job was reclaimed by its previous occupant, he applied to be Carnival's "assistant to the assistant to the assistant of the pastry chef" and got the job. Pastry turned out to be his calling.

"I never thought I was going to be doing it for the rest of my life, but this is where all my creativity comes out," he told me as we mixed the pecan filling for the tart crusts I had just massacred. "I just imagine them. I don't even taste them a lot of the time. I just give them to other people."

In addition to the pecan tarts, which he planned to serve with butterscotch sauce and mascarpone cream, the menu for that night included Ruby Red grapefruit sorbet with citrus compote and quince purée; warm chocolate soufflé with brandied cherry-pecan soup; the crepes; and a cinnamon-fennel crème brûlée with a pineapple, thyme, and lime compote.

But first came the tarts, which I needed to finish making. "Just put like a spoonful in the middle of each crust," August instructed. It sounded straightforward enough, but even that task was harder than I expected. I have fairly good hand-eye coordination, but somehow I missed the center of the tart tin with my spoonful of pecan goo more often than I hit it, so I had to go back and even out the level of filling over and over again.

One of the reasons this was so troubling was that it highlighted a major contradiction in my personality: I have a gigantic sweet tooth, but I'm basically incapable of making a dessert. In recent years I'd taken to just buying ice cream and cookies or serving somebody else's pie. When we had friends coming over and they asked what to bring, I always said dessert. A few times I'd tried to fool myself into thinking I could follow a cake recipe as easily as one for pork loin, but it wasn't true. The last time I'd baked a cake it had not, as Sarah would have said, ended well.

My brother-in-law's birthday is December 25, and after years of watching it get eclipsed by Christmas festivities, I wanted to do something in his honor besides arbitrarily writing "This one's for your birthday" on half of his presents. I would bake him a cake. I consulted with my closest friend, an expert baker, who gave me a recipe ("foolproof") that I followed to the letter. The cake looked perfect when it came out of the oven, but when I went into the kitchen about half an hour later, I noticed it had sunk in the middle. So I flipped it over, frosted it, and went about my business. By the time we had eaten our roast goose and cabbage and potatoes and the floor was strewn with wrapping paper, I had put the incident out of my mind. Then I went to get the cake and discovered that, thanks to its leaden center, it had cratered just as deeply in the opposite direction. It tasted delicious, and no one else seemed to mind its appearance, but the whole incident had scared me off ever trying again.

With that fiasco in mind, I decided that standing next to August and handing him plates and spoons was the safest thing to do for the remainder of the shift. Dinner service went off without a hitch, and though I didn't do much to help, I watched keenly, trying to learn something about baking for future reference. It was almost Jules's birthday, and a cake, obviously, was in order.

The one great exception to my failure as a maker of sweets up to that point was a boiled frosting so specific to my family that it didn't even have a name. My mother had made it for my sister and me when we were children (it was actually half a recipe from an old cookbook she had, but I didn't learn that until I was in my twenties), and now we made it for our own children and for each other whenever we were together on a birthday.

"Are you going to make the frosting?" I would ask my sister when one of her kids had a birthday.

"Do you think we should make the frosting?" she would ask me when our mother's birthday was coming around.

Though we knew there were plenty of other frostings in the world, we never even considered being disloyal to the one we knew best, which was made of a deathly sweet combination of sugar, corn syrup (that is, more sugar), and egg whites. So it was that I found myself on the morning of Jules's second birthday with a pot containing these ingredients on the stove and a candy thermometer at hand to test the temperature of the boiling mixture. I had armed myself with a cake mix to avoid the cratering problem, but I was not going to skimp on family tradition, even if applewood was exposing me to all kinds of new frosting secrets. When the liquid reached two hundred and forty-two degrees, I beat it into a bowl of egg whites I had whipped until they stood up in peaks. Earlier I had baked two chocolate layers, and now I stacked them with a layer of white goo in between to hold them together and a coating of shiny white all over the outside. In red frosting on the top, I wrote, disbelievingly, "JULES IS 2."

Family and friends gathered around the dinner table and sang as Noah brought the cake from the kitchen. Jules blew out the big numeral-two candle.

"Are you going to have cake?" Noah asked him.

"Yeah," he replied, wide-eyed.

When the plates were passed around, Jules picked off his frosting to eat and left the cake, but I counted it as a victory not only for tradition but for progress. The frosting was pure sugar, but it was something new.

I spent the next month at the pastry station, trying to figure out why things that seemed simple when August did them were absolutely beyond me. I mixed and whisked and cut out tart crusts, but mostly I stood by and watched. He made individual pineapple upside-down cakes with salted caramel (I sliced the pineapple). He made white wine–poached apples with sweet ricotta cheese and cinnamon streusel (I made the poaching liquid and set the apples in the pot to cook). He made espresso bread pudding with white chocolate ganache (I cut up the bread and dumped it in the pan) and almond poppyseed cake with blood orange frosting (I squeezed the oranges and served as official taster). In between, he made batches and batches of chocolate chip cookies, tiny and light, which appeared to be made of exactly the same ingredients *I* used to make chocolate chip cookies, but which were not like my cookies at all.

"Why are these so good when you make them and so not

good when I do?" I wondered aloud one day after popping one practically straight from the oven into my mouth.

"Because I've already made every mistake you can make," he answered, handing me another. "Twice."

Ordinarily I would have taken some comfort from this, but as soon as he said it I realized that I didn't need any. I was no longer obsessed with what I did or didn't know how to do with food. I knew enough.

Up front they were making crispy kale (baked in the oven with salt on a sheet tray—a big hit with Jules when I tried it at home), a tomato tapenade, and a beautiful salad made of a fluttery chiffonade of long, thin strips of chard, green with a smattering of magenta. All of these dishes seemed, somewhat to my surprise, like things it might occur to me to make at home, though I thought I might cook the chard instead of serving it raw as a salad. I had a lot of ideas. Pastry was different, of course, since you had to know all the ratios of liquid to dry ingredients to make the recipes work; August constantly consulted a food-splattered notebook and various crumpled-looking pieces of paper on which he had written recipes. But even my inadequacy as a pastry chef didn't seem vitally important. I could always buy dessert.

I mixed up the next batch of cookie dough and we scurried around until dinner service began, weighing out chocolate and checking the sorbet in the freezer to make sure it was hard enough.

It was slow at pastry the first part of the night—everyone seemed to be lingering over their entrées and then deciding they were too full for dessert—and August was bored and slightly grumpy. Because we had nothing to do during dinner service but put together dessert plates when people ordered them (which was great fun and involved dribbling and splashing sauces onto plates as decoration and popping little cakes and crumbles and bread puddings into the toaster oven to warm them up), we stood around waiting for the servers to come back and stick dessert tickets on the rail above the pastry station. "I'd go crazy if it was like this all the time," August grumbled. "Let's make truffles."

So we stood at the back of the kitchen, dipping melon ballers into a deep hotel pan of chilled truffle mixture made of chocolate and heavy cream, over and over and over. Then around eight-thirty, just when I thought my hand was going to fall off from pressing the utensil into the hardened chocolate, the first dessert order came in: espresso-flavored bread pudding. Action!

I took a round cookie cutter about two inches high over to the speed rack, a tall, open-sided shelving frame with runners for sliding in baking trays and hotel pans, used for easily accessible storage and also as a place to put hot trays for cooling. Pulling the hotel pan of bread pudding partway out so that I could reach into it, I pressed the cutter down into the slightly crispy, uneven top, twisted it a few times, then pulled it out with a perfect short cylinder of bread pudding inside it. I pushed the pudding out with a spoon onto a small metal sizzle platter used for heating and handed it to August, who stuck it in the toaster oven. After about five minutes he grabbed the platter out with a side towel, dusted the top of the pudding with powdered sugar, and transferred it to a plate with a spatula. I dipped a spoon into the quart of white-chocolate ganache sauce sitting on the counter, then drizzled some onto the plate in a circle around the bread pudding and zigzagged a bit of it over the top. Next I stacked some chopped pecans on top of the pudding, and voilà! August marched the plate to the front of the room and set it on the counter closest to the dining room door, with the ticket underneath it. Walking back toward me, he had a look of pleased relief on his face. Something was happening at last.

This was how nights on the pastry station unfolded: All the pressure was in the afternoon, and August came in around ten A.M. a few times a week to get started and to have full use of the ovens before everyone else got in and started filling them with squash or potatoes. By the time dinner service rolled around, if everything had gone well, he had nothing to do but wait impatiently and assemble. There wasn't even any fire involved, which made pastry the coolest station, if the least adrenaline-filled. When things were really dull, August spent the first few hours of dinner service testing new recipes to keep from going nuts.

One evening at about six o'clock, before anyone had come in to eat, he passed around some almond cookies he had just made for the first time. They were crisp and light on the outside and soft and slightly chewy on the inside, and they melted the moment they hit your tongue.

"Soooo good," David said happily. "How'd you think of these?"

August started laughing. "I have no idea! I found this recipe under my bed when I was looking for the remote control." He didn't even know how long it had been there. I pondered this information while eating another half-dozen cookies, trying to remember if I'd ever found anything other than dust bunnies or Jules's miniature skateboards under my own bed. I was obviously never going to be a pastry chef.

Still, it was amazing to behold one up close. On another slow evening, August started experimenting with various kinds of brownies. "No one is ordering dessert," he sighed, looking enviously at the grill and fish stations, which were being slammed with orders. Then about five minutes later, he went to the oven, pulled out a pan, and brought it over to pastry. It was filled with something crusty and caramel-colored.

"What is that?" I asked.

"White and dark chocolate macadamia nut brownies," he said, his frustrations forgotten. He patted the top of the cake gently, as if it were a baby, cut a small slice, and sniffed it appreciatively before putting it in his mouth. His face relaxed with pleasure. "Do you have any idea how much I love my job?" he said in a small, happy voice, looking sideways at me.

"Even when you're in a bad mood?"

"Even when I'm in a bad mood," he replied, sliding his brownie creation onto the speed rack to cool. It was as though everything boring or stressful about the day had never happened.

August let me plate all the desserts that night, and before long I had mastered the toasting and drizzling and arrang-

ing. I couldn't invent a dessert, but I could plate one with
the best of them, and he saw this development as the rare
opportunity it was. The next day at around five-thirty, when
everything was set up for dinner service, he took advantage
of my presence and left early. He had been in the kitchen until midnight the night before and back at nine A.M. to do his
prep work, and he was exhausted. On the menu that night
were the new brownies, served with mascarpone cream and
coconut *dulce de leche,* the last of the Ruby Red grapefruit
sorbet with roasted apple purée and citrus salad, a pineapple rice pudding, a warm chocolate soufflé with quince purée and hazelnuts, and a sweet corn pudding with shortbread
cookie crumble and sweet cream—and he was trusting me to
make them all look good in his name.

All I had to go on was the note he had left for me, written on a paper towel and stuck into the ticket rail above the
pastry counter.

—More corn pudding and rice pudding downstairs.
—corn behind the animals
—need to keep putting on the mini-oven
—my cell [here he had written his phone number]
—I

I never figured out what he'd meant to write on that last
line, but I made it through the evening anyway. Up front
David and Greg were experimenting with breadmaking to
fill the time before tickets started coming in, but I had no
part in that. I was on pastry, and I felt I shouldn't leave my
appointed post. As they fired fish and meat, I warmed up

268 · EATING FOR BEGINNERS

chocolate soufflés in the toaster oven and put each one on a plate with a small pile of toasted hazelnuts on top and a half-moon smear of quince purée next to it. I pulled parfait glasses of pudding out of the lowboy and piped cream onto them in neat little spirals, then dusted them with cookie crumbs. I went down to the walk-in for more corn pudding and had to shove my body against a pig to get at it, just as I had a year earlier to reach the bacon. Then I took the pudding up to the kitchen and plated some more. I drizzled dulce de leche and spooned citrus salad. I ate constantly, sugary bite after sugary bite, and went home wired and happy.

The next afternoon when I walked into work, August, already in his chef's jacket and pants, Che Guevara hat on his head, was standing in front of the counter at the pastry station with a blank look on his face.

"What's wrong?" I asked, feeling anxious about my performance the night before. Had I inadvertently mis-drizzled or stacked too precariously?

"I need to do something with bread," August said, zombie-like. He gestured toward the speed rack, where all the bread left over from the previous night's dinner service lay on a sheet tray under Saran Wrap. Nothing went unused in the kitchen, so it had been given to him to transform into a dessert. "I'm looking for something to do with bread pudding," he said again, turning to me this time. "Let's go downstairs."

I started to protest that I certainly wasn't going to be the one who figured out what to do, but he silenced me. We walked down to the shelves of dry goods in front of the walk-in, me still in my street clothes, and stood there pondering the boxes of nuts and dried fruit and beans and seasonings.

Without really thinking, I said, "How about prunes?"

August's eyes lit up. "Yeah. That's going to be good."

Reaching for a big plastic bag of prunes, he told me, "Write down that today you invented the Melanie Bread Pudding."

I stayed downstairs for a minute or two after he'd headed up with the prunes, changing into my chef's jacket and basking in the glow of my first-ever menu idea. Then I tore up to the kitchen to put it into execution.

The bread pudding came out spectacularly. It seemed like a good note to go out on, and I decided that evening that it was time to turn my attention to writing instead of cooking.

Walking home that last night, I suddenly realized I was looking forward to seeing what Jules might eat the following day. He was into all kinds of things that late spring—lots of melon (I forgave him for it) and anything sour or spicy. He was adding fresh fruits and vegetables at an amazing clip as they became available, and I was beginning to think that rather than having a totally undeveloped palate, he might have the kind I had gone to applewood to learn about: he ate what was in season, not because he knew he was supposed to, but because it tasted good. He had never even sampled a frozen vegetable, but now that fresh ones were abundant at the farmers' market, he was choosing and trying new foods each week. Any cheese other than cream cheese was still off limits, and he hadn't gone anywhere near a piece of pasta or meat, or even a hot dog, but I couldn't quite remember why those details had seemed so important to me.

A few months passed, during which I sat at my desk and began writing this book. Often, around six o'clock, I paused for a minute in whatever I was doing, whether it was typing on my computer or getting dinner together for Jules, distracted by a longing to be part of what I knew was going on in the kitchen down the street. I wondered what produce the summer—and the Angello's truck—had brought to the restaurant, and what the chefs were making out of it. I missed the sense of collective anticipation at the beginning of each dinner shift and, if not the sweat, certainly Greg's salsa verde. At applewood I had been given a larger sense of the world that had to do not only with food but with community, and I felt the absence keenly.

But I also found that community in other places—the same places where I had once felt utterly confused. One of my local markets now stocked produce from Angello's, and I was thrilled to discover Lucky Dog lettuce and carrots along with other locally grown produce, all of which I bought without a clue as to what I would do with it. On weekends I went to the farmers' market and purchased with abandon. One stand sold a mix of salad greens that was as addictive as it was expensive, but I now understood exactly where my money was going and why I wanted to spend it there instead of on a bag of organic mesclun at the supermarket. Cato Corner had a cheese stand, where I happily indulged my craving for Bloomsday, and there was a fish stand that sold dayboat scallops and other local fish (by midsummer I no longer felt queasy at the mere mention of boats).

I didn't know all of these farmers and fishermen and meat purveyors personally, but I now knew where they came from, philosophically if not literally. I had entered their lives and found them less different from my own life than I'd expected; out of this understanding had come the balance I'd been looking for.

Though I missed the restaurant, it was nice to be home for dinner every night. As the summer rolled on, we sat in the dining room in the evenings with the windows open, listening to kids playing in the park, sharing whatever we could with Jules while we ate, which was still not all that much. I had ceased to worry about what he ate, not because he had suddenly turned into an omnivore, but because I no longer felt guilty about him not being one.

On one of these nights I roasted a chicken and we ate it with coleslaw and corn on the cob. Jules was feasting on his corn when Noah asked me if the chefs ever made chicken at applewood.

"Only for family meal," I said, picking up a chicken leg in my fingers. "David told me he had a recipe he loved on the menu when they first opened, but no one ever ordered chicken, so he stopped putting it on."

"Too bad," said Noah. "I like chicken."

Jules put down his corn. "I like chicken," he announced.

Noah and I exchanged a knowing look. We had heard it all before.

"I want chicken," Jules insisted.

Noah passed him the plate.

He took a leg. Then he took a bite, and all three of us dug into our dinner.

❖ Under the Bed Almond Cookies

1 pound almond paste
½ cup sugar
1½ cups egg whites

1. Preheat oven to 350 degrees.
2. Cream almond paste and sugar together.
3. Add egg whites.
4. Drop mixture onto a cookie sheet in ball shapes about 1½–2 inches in diameter, making sure they do not touch one another and have room to spread.
5. Bake for 15 minutes or until golden brown.

Makes about 3 dozen cookies.

❖ Melanie's Prune Bread Pudding

2 cups dried prunes
2 tablespoons vanilla
1–2 teaspoons ground cinnamon
a pinch of freshly grated nutmeg
1½ teaspoons salt
1 loaf good white bread, cut into cubes and left to dry
   out overnight

½ pound (2 sticks) butter, melted

3 cups heavy cream

4 whole eggs and 5 egg yolks

1 cup sour cream

½ cup sugar

1. Preheat oven to 350 degrees.

2. Put prunes in a saucepan with the vanilla, cinnamon, nutmeg, and salt. Add water to about two inches above the prunes. Cook down over medium heat to the tops of the prunes.

3. Strain the prunes and purée them in a food processor or blender.

4. Place the bread cubes in a bowl and pour the melted butter over them, tossing to make sure they're all buttered.

5. Mix together the cream, eggs, and sour cream in another bowl.

6. Add the prune purée and the sugar to the cream/egg mixture. If the mixture is not totally liquid, add more cream.

7. Place the bread cubes in an unbuttered oblong pan, then pour the prune/cream mixture over them. The bread should be completely soaked.

8. Cover the pan with foil and bake for 1 hour.

9. After an hour, remove the foil and return the pan to the oven just long enough to brown the top of the bread pudding. Let cool before cutting into squares to serve.

Serves about 6, depending on how big you cut the pieces.

Acknowledgments

The people in these pages who let me into their lives, showed me the joys and difficulties of their work, introduced me to their children, and took me seriously when I was under-dressed for the job at hand, did so because I came to them through David and Laura Shea, whose good word is all their friends and acquaintances need to throw open their doors without question. I (along with most of the people I know) am still marveling that the Sheas allowed me into their res-taurant and let me cook food just because I asked them if I could. It is because of their fearlessness, patience, and good humor that *Eating for Beginners* exists.

I an indebted to Mark Gillman and Elizabeth MacAlister of Cato Corner Farm; Richard and Holley Giles of Lucky Dog Organics; Joe Angello of Angello's Distributing; Lydia Ratcliff of Lovejoy Brook Farm and Fancy Meats from Ver-mont; Lucy Georgeff and Oliver Owen, now of East Hill Farm and Pastured Meats from East Hill Farm; and Kevin

Wark and Mike Lohr. Each of them gave me experiences and wisdom far beyond the scope of this book and was incredibly good company, too.

Thank you to Greg, who more than anyone but David was stuck with me on the line and somehow always behaved as though I belonged there; to Liza, Sarah, and August, who all taught me an enormous amount and were fun to be around on top of it; and to the servers at applewood during my time there, who tolerated me in the kitchen even when their orders were a bit late to come out. A special thank you to Frank and another to Pete, who kept me in coffee and good spirits whenever my enthusiasm flagged.

I wouldn't be able to write a word without Brad McKee ever at the ready. I couldn't do it without MacKenzie Bezos, either. Thanks also to Patrick Keefe (still my fellow neurotic) and Liz Leber for reading various sections at various stages and urging me along. I am grateful to Wyatt Prunty not only for writing the miraculous "A Winter's Tale" but for graciously allowing me to reprint the lines here that have sustained me for a very long time.

Thank you to Christy Fletcher, whose head for both business and books (as well as many other things) I envy. As always, I'm amazed by my incalculable good fortune in counting Andrea Schulz as both editor and friend.

Without Noah Isenberg, I would be somewhere else entirely—somewhere far less rich and surprising—from where I am in life. To the lovely and astonishing Jules I owe more than I'll ever be able to write down.